3

Praise for Christmas Delights

A Collection of Christmas Recipes
Cookbook Delights Holiday Series Book 12

…"I turn to this cookbook time and time again to find new and creative ways to celebrate the season. *Christmas Delights Cookbook* delivers hundreds of recipes like your Mom and Grandma used to make; from delicious appetizers, drinks, and desserts, to mouth watering main dishes. It's a great guide to discovering the secrets to scrumptious cooking!

This cookbook has actually helped to bring my family closer together by showing me how to create festive settings that are memorable, complete with food that is most satisfying. When I read through these pages it puts me in the holiday mood anytime of year!"…

Kimberly Carter
Publicist

…"Praise to *Christmas Delights Cookbook* which has all the makings of a classic favorite. Now you too can prepare that dish that everyone wants the recipe for!

Author Karen Jean Matsko Hood presents a wide variety of holiday treats. This book will serve you well through every event, from the meet and greet, through the seven course meal.

Instead of the same routine, try something new and unexpected this year!"…

Ed Archambeault
Spokane, WA

Praise for Christmas Delights

A Collection of Christmas Recipes
Cookbook Delights Holiday Series Book 12

…"You will enjoy making all the tantalizing dishes that inhabit the 324 pages of *Christmas Delights Cookbook*. Your family will find it fascinating to learn about Christmas customs in other countries in the section "Christmas around the World" and about how to care for your poinsettia in the section "Caring for your Poinsettia." This book is full of facts, traditions, symbols, poetry, and so much more. *Christmas Delights Cookbook* promises to be an added family tradition and a keepsake for many happy years to come."…

Mary Scripture
Graphic Designer

… *"Christmas Delights Cookbook* is not only a cookbook, but a wealth of information about Christmas. It includes fascinating facts, folklore, history of Christmas, Christmas symbols, Christmas around the world, poetry, and traditions. It even includes information on caring for your poinsettia.

In addition to all this information it has a collection of over 250 recipes that are delicious, and will be enjoyed by your family and friends.

This is a great value for the price and makes a wonderful gift."…

Dr. James G. Hood
Editor

Christmas Delights

A Collection of Christmas Recipes
Cookbook Delights Holiday Series Book 12

Karen Jean Matsko Hood

Current and Future Cookbooks
By Karen Jean Matsko Hood

DELIGHTS SERIES
Almond Delights
Anchovy Delights
Apple Delights
Apricot Delights
Artichoke Delights
Asparagus Delights
Avocado Delights
Banana Delights
Barley Delights
Basil Delights
Bean Delights
Beef Delights
Beer Delights
Beet Delights
Blackberry Delights
Blueberry Delights
Bok Choy Delights
Boysenberry Delights
Brazil Nut Delights
Broccoli Delights
Brussels Sprouts Delights
Buffalo Berry Delights
Butter Delights
Buttermilk Delights
Cabbage Delights
Calamari Delights
Cantaloupe Delights
Caper Delights
Cardamom Delights
Carrot Delights
Cashew Delights
Cauliflower Delights
Celery Delights
Cheese Delights
Cherry Delights
Chestnut Delights
Chicken Delights
Chili Pepper Delights
Chive Delights

Chocolate Delights
Chokecherry Delights
Cilantro Delights
Cinnamon Delights
Clam Delights
Clementine Delights
Coconut Delights
Coffee Delights
Conch Delights
Corn Delights
Cottage Cheese Delights
Crab Delights
Cranberry Delights
Cucumber Delights
Cumin Delights
Curry Delights
Date Delights
Edamame Delights
Egg Delights
Eggplant Delights
Elderberry Delights
Endive Delights
Fennel Delights
Fig Delights
Filbert (Hazelnut) Delights
Fish Delights
Garlic Delights
Ginger Delights
Ginseng Delights
Goji Berry Delights
Grape Delights
Grapefruit Delights
Grapple Delights
Guava Delights
Ham Delights
Hamburger Delights
Herb Delights
Herbal Tea Delights
Honey Delights
Honeyberry Delights

Honeydew Delights
Horseradish Delights
Huckleberry Delights
Jalapeño Delights
Jerusalem Artichoke Delights
Jicama Delights
Kale Delights
Kiwi Delights
Kohlrabi Delights
Lavender Delights
Leek Delights
Lemon Delights
Lentil Delights
Lettuce Delights
Lime Delights
Lingonberry Delights
Lobster Delights
Loganberry Delights
Macadamia Nut Delights
Mango Delights
Marionberry Delights
Milk Delights
Mint Delights
Miso Delights
Mushroom Delights
Mussel Delights
Nectarine Delights
Oatmeal Delights
Olive Delights
Onion Delights
Orange Delights
Oregon Berry Delights
Oyster Delights
Papaya Delights
Parsley Delights
Parsnip Delights
Pea Delights
Peach Delights
Peanut Delights
Pear Delights
Pecan Delights
Pepper Delights
Persimmon Delights
Pine Nut Delights
Pineapple Delights

Pistachio Delights
Plum Delights
Pomegranate Delights
Pomelo Delights
Popcorn Delights
Poppy Seed Delights
Pork Delights
Potato Delights
Prickly Pear Cactus Delights
Prune Delights
Pumpkin Delights
Quince Delights
Quinoa Delights
Radish Delights
Raisin Delights
Raspberry Delights
Rhubarb Delights
Rice Delights
Rose Delights
Rosemary Delights
Rutabaga Delights
Salmon Delights
Salmonberry Delights
Salsify Delights
Savory Delights
Scallop Delights
Seaweed Delights
Serviceberry Delights
Sesame Delights
Shallot Delights
Shrimp Delights
Soybean Delights
Spinach Delights
Squash Delights
Star Fruit Delights
Strawberry Delights
Sunflower Seed Delights
Sweet Potato Delights
Swiss Chard Delights
Tangerine Delights
Tapioca Delights
Tayberry Delights
Tea Delights
Teaberry Delights
Thimbleberry Delights

Tofu Delights
Tomatillo Delights
Tomato Delights
Trout Delights
Truffle Delights
Tuna Delights
Turkey Delights
Turmeric Delights
Turnip Delights
Vanilla Delights
Walnut Delights
Wasabi Delights
Watermelon Delights
Wheat Delights
Wild Rice Delights
Yam Delights
Yogurt Delights
Zucchini Delights

CITY DELIGHTS
Chicago Delights
Coeur d'Alene Delights
Great Falls Delights
Honolulu Delights
Minneapolis Delights
Phoenix Delights
Portland Delights
Sandpoint Delights
Scottsdale Delights
Seattle Delights
Spokane Delights
St. Cloud Delights

FOSTER CARE
Foster Children Cookbook
  and Activity Book
Foster Children's Favorite
  Recipes
Holiday Cookbook for
  Foster Families

**GENERAL THEME
  DELIGHTS**
Appetizer Delights
Baby Food Delights
Barbeque Delights

Beer-Making Delights
Beverage Delights
Biscotti Delights
Bisque Delights
Blender Delights
Bread Delights
Bread Maker Delights
Breakfast Delights
Brunch Delights
Cake Delights
Campfire Food Delights
Candy Delights
Canned Food Delights
Cast Iron Delights
Cheesecake Delights
Chili Delights
Chowder Delights
Cocktail Delights
College Cooking Delights
Comfort Food Delights
Cookie Delights
Cooking for One Delights
Cooking for Two Delights
Cracker Delights
Crepe Delights
Crockpot Delights
Dairy Delights
Dehydrated Food Delights
Dessert Delights
Dinner Delights
Dutch Oven Delights
Foil Delights
Fondue Delights
Food Processor Delights
Fried Food Delights
Frozen Food Delights
Fruit Delights
Gelatin Delights
Grilled Delights
Hiking Food Delights
Ice Cream Delights
Juice Delights
Kid's Delights
Kosher Diet Delights
Liqueur-Making Delights

Liqueurs and Spirits Delights
Lunch Delights
Marinade Delights
Microwave Delights
Milk Shake and Malt Delights
Panini Delights
Pasta Delights
Pesto Delights
Phyllo Delights
Pickled Food Delights
Picnic Food Delights
Pizza Delights
Preserved Delights
Pudding and Custard Delights
Quiche Delights
Quick Mix Delights
Rainbow Delights
Salad Delights
Salsa Delights
Sandwich Delights
Sea Vegetable Delights
Seafood Delights
Smoothie Delights
Snack Delights
Soup Delights
Supper Delights
Tart Delights
Torte Delights
Tropical Delights
Vegan Delights
Vegetable Delights
Vegetarian Delights
Vinegar Delights
Wildflower Delights
Wine Delights
Winemaking Delights
Wok Delights

GIFTS-IN-A-JAR SERIES
Beverage Gifts-in-a-Jar
Christmas Gifts-in-a-Jar
Cookie Gifts-in-a-Jar
Gifts-in-a-Jar
Gifts-in-a-Jar Catholic
Gifts-in-a-Jar Christian

Holiday Gifts-in-a-Jar
Soup Gifts-in-a-Jar

HEALTH-RELATED DELIGHTS
Achalasia Diet Delights
Adrenal Health Diet Delights
Anti-Acid Reflux Diet Delights
Anti-Cancer Diet Delights
Anti-Inflammation Diet
   Delights
Anti-Stress Diet Delights
Arthritis Delights
Bone Health Diet Delights
Diabetic Diet Delights
Diet for Pink Delights
Fibromyalgia Diet Delights
Gluten-Free Diet Delights
Healthy Breath Diet Delights
Healthy Digestion Diet
   Delights
Healthy Heart Diet Delights
Healthy Skin Diet Delights
Healthy Teeth Diet Delights
High-Fiber Diet Delights
High-Iodine Diet Delights
High-Protein Diet Delights
Immune Health Diet Delights
Kidney Health Diet Delights
Lactose-Free Diet Delights
Liquid Diet Delights
Liver Health Diet Delights
Low-Calorie Diet Delights
Low-Carb Diet Delights
Low-Fat Diet Delights
Low-Sodium Diet Delights
Low-Sugar Diet Delights
Lymphoma Health Support
   Diet Delights
Multiple Sclerosis Healthy
   Diet Delights
No Flour No Sugar Diet
   Delights
Organic Food Delights
pH-Friendly Diet Delights

9

Pregnancy Diet Delights
Raw Food Diet Delights
Sjögren's Syndrome Diet
  Delights
Soft Food Diet Delights
Thyroid Health Diet Delights

HOLIDAY DELIGHTS
Christmas Delights
Easter Delights
Father's Day Delights
Fourth of July Delights
Grandparent's Day Delights
Halloween Delights
Hanukkah Delights
Labor Day Weekend Delights
Memorial Day Weekend
  Delights
Mother's Day Delights
New Year's Delights
St. Patrick's Day Delights
Thanksgiving Delights
Valentine Delights

HOOD AND MATSKO
FAMILY FAVORITES
Hood and Matsko Family
  Appetizers Cookbook
Hood and Matsko Family
  Beverages Cookbook
Hood and Matsko Family
  Breads and Rolls Cookbook
Hood and Matsko Family
  Breakfasts Cookbook
Hood and Matsko Family
  Cakes Cookbook
Hood and Matsko Family
  Candies Cookbook
Hood and Matsko Family
  Casseroles Cookbook
Hood and Matsko Family
  Cookies Cookbook
Hood and Matsko Family
  Desserts Cookbook
Hood and Matsko Family

Dressings, Sauces, and
  Condiments Cookbook
Hood and Matsko Family
  Ethnic Cookbook
Hood and Matsko Family
  Jams, Jellies, Syrups,
  Preserves, and Conserves
Hood and Matsko Family
  Main Dishes Cookbook
Hood and Matsko Family,
  Pies Cookbook
Hood and Matsko Family
  Preserving Cookbook
Hood and Matsko Family
  Salads and Salad Dressings
Hood and Matsko Family
  Side Dishes Cookbook
Hood and Matsko Family
  Vegetable Cookbook
Hood and Matsko Family,
  Aunt Katherine's Recipe
  Collection, Vol. I-II
Hood and Matsko Family,
  Grandma Bert's Recipe
  Collection, Vol. I-IV

HOOD AND MATSKO
FAMILY HOLIDAY
Hood and Matsko Family
  Favorite Birthday Recipes
Hood and Matsko Family
  Favorite Christmas Recipes
Hood and Matsko Family
  Favorite Christmas Sweets
Hood and Matsko Family
  Easter Cookbook
Hood and Matsko Family
  Favorite Thanksgiving Recipes

INTERNATIONAL
DELIGHTS
African Delights
African American Delights
Australian Delights
Austrian Delights

Brazilian Delights
Canadian Delights
Chilean Delights
Chinese Delights
Czechoslovakian Delights
English Delights
Ethiopian Delights
Fijian Delights
French Delights
German Delights
Greek Delights
Hungarian Delights
Icelandic Delights
Indian Delights
Irish Delights
Italian Delights
Korean Delights
Mexican Delights
Native American Delights
Polish Delights
Russian Delights
Scottish Delights
Slovenian Delights
Swedish Delights
Thai Delights
The Netherlands Delights
Yugoslavian Delights
Zambian Delights

REGIONAL DELIGHTS
Glacier National Park Delights
Northwest Regional Delights
Oregon Coast Delights
Schweitzer Mountain Delights
Southwest Regional Delights
Tropical Delights
Washington Wine Country
  Delights
Wine Delights of Walla
  Walla Wineries
Yellowstone National Park
  Delights

SEASONAL DELIGHTS
Autumn Harvest Delights

Spring Harvest Delights
Summer Harvest Delights
Winter Harvest Delights

SPECIAL EVENTS
DELIGHTS
Birthday Delights
Coffee Klatch Delights
Super Bowl Delights
Tea Time Delights

STATE DELIGHTS
Alaska Delights
Arizona Delights
Georgia Delights
Hawaii Delights
Idaho Delights
Illinois Delights
Iowa Delights
Louisiana Delights
Minnesota Delights
Montana Delights
North Dakota Delights
Oregon Delights
South Dakota Delights
Texas Delights
Washington Delights

U.S. TERRITORIES
DELIGHTS
Cruzan Delights
U.S. Virgin Island Delights

MISCELLANEOUS
COOKBOOKS
Getaway Studio Cookbook
The Soup Doctor's Cookbook

BILINGUAL DELIGHTS
SERIES
Apple Delights, English-
  French Edition
Apple Delights, English-
  Russian Edition
Apple Delights, English-
  Spanish Edition

Huckleberry Delights,
  English-French Edition
Huckleberry Delights,
  English-Russian Edition
Huckleberry Delights,
  English-Spanish Edition

CATHOLIC DELIGHTS
SERIES
Apple Delights Catholic
Coffee Delights Catholic
Easter Delights Catholic
Huckleberry Delights Catholic
Tea Delights Catholic

CATHOLIC BILINGUAL
DELIGHTS SERIES
Apple Delights Catholic,
  English-French Edition
Apple Delights Catholic,
  English-Russian Edition
Apple Delights Catholic,
  English-Spanish Edition
Huckleberry Delights
  Catholic, English-Spanish
  Edition

CHRISTIAN DELIGHTS
SERIES
Apple Delights Christian
Coffee Delights Christian
Easter Delights Christian
Huckleberry Delights Christian
Tea Delights Christian

CHRISTIAN BILINGUAL
DELIGHTS SERIES
Apple Delights Christian,
  English-French Edition
Apple Delights Christian,
  English-Russian Edition
Apple Delights Christian,
  English-Spanish Edition
Huckleberry Delights
  Christian, English-Spanish
  Edition

FUNDRAISING
COOKBOOKS
Ask about our fundraising
  cookbooks to help raise
  funds for your organization.

The above books are also available in bilingual versions. Please contact Whispering Pine Press International, Inc., for details.

Please note that some books are future books and are currently in production. Please contact us for availability date. Prices are subject to change without notice.

The above list of books is not all-inclusive. For a complete list please visit our website or contact us at:

Whispering Pine Press International, Inc.
Your Northwest Book Publishing Company
P.O. Box 214
Spokane Valley, WA 99037-0214 USA
Phone: (509) 928-8700 | Fax: (509) 922-9949
Email: sales@whisperingpinepress.com
Publisher Websites: www.WhisperingPinePress.com
www.WhisperingPinePressBookstore.com
Blog: www.WhisperingPinePressBlog.com

Christmas Delights
A Collection of Christmas Recipes
Cookbook Delights Holiday Series Book 12

Karen Jean Matsko Hood

Published by:

Whispering Pine Press International, Inc.
Your Northwest Book Publishing Company
P.O. Box 214
Spokane Valley, WA 99037-0214 USA
Phone: (509) 928-8700 | Fax: (509) 922-9949
Email: sales@whisperingpinepress.com
Publisher Websites: www.WhisperingPinePress.com
www.WhisperingPinePressBookstore.com
Blog: www.WhisperingPinePressBlog.com
SAN 253-200X
Printed in the U.S.A.

Published by Whispering Pine Press International, Inc.
P.O. Box 214
Spokane Valley, Washington 99037-0214 USA

For sales outside the United States, please contact the Whispering Pine Press International, Inc., International Sales Department.

Book and Cover Design by Artistic Design Service, Inc.
P.O. Box 1782
Spokane Valley, WA 99037-1782 USA
www.ArtisticDesignService.com

Library of Congress Number (LCCN): 2014901415

Hood, Karen Jean Matsko
    Title: Christmas Delights Cookbook: A Collection of Christmas Recipes: Cookbook Delights Holiday Series Book 12

    p.   cm.

ISBN: 978-1-59434-156-4   case bound
ISBN: 978-1-59434-157-1   perfect bound
ISBN: 978-1-59434-158-8   spiral bound
ISBN: 978-1-59434-159-5   comb bound
ISBN: 978-1-59434-162-5   E-PDF
ISBN: 978-1-59210-391-1   E-PUB
ISBN: 978-1-59434-867-9   E-PRC

First Edition: January 2014
1. Cookery (Christmas Delights Cookbook: A Collection of Christmas Recipes: *Cookbook Delights Holiday Series Book 12*)   1. Title

Christmas Delights Cookbook
A Collection of Christmas Recipes
Cookbook Delights Holiday Series Book 12

Gift Inscription

To:_____

From: _____

Date: _____

Special Message: _____

_____

_____

_____

_____

_____

_____

_____

*It is always nice to receive a personal note to
create a special memory.*

www.ChristmasDelights.net
www.WhisperingPinePress.com
www.WhisperingPinePressBookstore.com

Dedications

To my husband and best friend, Jim.

To our seventeen children: Gabriel, Brianne Kristina and her husband Moulik Vinodkumar Kothari, Marissa Kimberly and her husband Kevin Matthew Franck, Janelle Karina and her husband Paul Joseph Turcotte, Mikayla Karlene, Kyler James, Kelsey Katrina, Corbin Joel, Caleb Jerome, Keisha Kalani Hiwot, Devontay Joshua, Kianna Karielle Selam, Rosy Kiara, Mercedes Katherine, Jasmine Khalia Wengel, Cheyenne Krystal, and Annalise Kaylee Marie.

To our grandchildren and foster grandchildren: Courtney, Lorenzo, and Leah.

To my brother, Stephen, and his wife, Karen.

To my husband's ten siblings: Gary, Colleen, John, Dan, Mary, Ray, Ann, Teresa, Barbara, Agnes, and their families.

In loving memory of my mom, who passed away in 2007; my dad, who passed away in 1976; and my sister, Sandy, who passed away due to multiple sclerosis in 1999.

To Sandy's three sons: Monte, Bradley, and Derek. To Monte's wife, Sarah, and their children: Liam, Alice, Charlie, and Samuel. To Bradley's wife, Shawnda, and their children: Anton, Isaac, and Isabel.

To our foster children past and present: Krystal, Sara, Rebecca, Janice, Devontay Joshua, Mercedes Katherine, Zha'Nell, Makia, Onna, Cheyenne Krystal, Onna Marie, Nevaeh, and Zada, our future foster children, and all foster children everywhere.

To the Court Appointed Special Advocate (CASA) Volunteer Program in the judicial system which benefits abused and neglected children.

To the Literacy Campaign dedicated to promoting literacy throughout the world.

Acknowledgements

The author would like to acknowledge all those individuals who helped me during my time in writing this book. Appreciation is extended for all their support and effort they put into this project.

Deep gratitude and profound thanks are owed to my husband, Jim, for giving freely of his time and encouragement during this project. Also, thanks are owed to my children Gabriel, Brianne Kristina and her husband Moulik Vinodkumar Kothari, Marissa Kimberly and her husband Kevin Matthew Franck, Janelle Karina and her husband Paul Joseph Turcotte, Mikayla Karlene, Kyler James, Kelsey Katrina, Corbin Joel, Caleb Jerome, Keisha Kalani Hiwot, Devontay Joshua, Kianna Karielle Selam, Rosy Kiara, Mercedes Katherine, Jasmine Khalia Wengel, Cheyenne Krystal, and Annalise Kaylee Marie. All of these persons inspire my writing.

Thanks are due to Beverly Koerperich and Sharron Thompson for their assistance in editing and typing this manuscript for publication. Thanks go to Artistic Design Service, Inc. for their assistance in formatting and providing a graphic design of this manuscript for publication. This project could not have been completed without them.

Many thanks are due to members of my family, all of whom were very supportive during the time it took to complete this project. Their patience and support are greatly appreciated.

Christmas Delights Cookbook

Table of Contents

Christmas Delights Cookbook
A Collection of Christmas Recipes
Cookbook Delights Holiday Series Book 12

Introduction

Christmas is both a religious and special family holiday. What a perfect occasion upon which to design a cookbook. The recipes in this book have been collected around the themes, colors, and symbols of Christmas. These recipes are great for Christmas, but can also be used every day. We hope you enjoy reading it as well as trying out all the recipes.

This cookbook is designed for easy use and is organized into convenient alphabetical sections such as: appetizers and dips; beverages; breads and rolls; breakfasts; cakes; candies; cookies; desserts; dressings, sauces, and condiments; jams, jellies, and syrups; main dishes; pies; preserving; salads; side dishes; soups; and wine and spirits.

As a poet, I found it enjoyable to color this cookbook with poetry so that readers could savor the metaphorical richness of Christmas as well as the literal flavors of the holiday recipes. Do enjoy your reading about Christmas, but most importantly, have fun with those you care about while you are cooking.

Be sure to look at the list of current and future cookbooks for other titles in the Delights Series of books that you might desire. If you do not find the subject you are looking for, please email us with your suggestion for consideration in our list of current and future cookbooks. You may email us at sales@whisperingpinepress.com.

Following is a collection of information and recipes gathered and modified to bring you *Christmas Delights Cookbook: A Collection of Christmas Recipes, Cookbook Delights Series,* by Karen Jean Matsko Hood.

Christmas Delights Cookbook
A Collection of Christmas Recipes
Cookbook Delights Holiday Series Book 12

Poinsettia
Botanical Classification

Poinsettia Botanical Classification

Kingdom: *Plantae*
Division: *Magnoliophyta*
Class: *Magnoliopsida*
Order: *Malpighiales*
Family: *Euphorbiaceae*
Genus: *Euphorbia*
Species: *E. pulcherrima*
Binomial name: *Euphorbia pulcherrima*

Poinsettias are flowers found in the wild in deciduous tropical forests at moderate elevations from southern Sinaloa down the entire Pacific coast of Mexico to Chiapas and into Guatemala. It is also found in some parts of central southern Mexico in the hot, seasonally dry forests in Guerrero, Oaxaca, and a few localities in Guatemala.

They are named after Joel Roberts Poinsett, the first United States ambassador to Mexico, who introduced the plant in the United States in 1825. The Mexican poinsettia is known as the Christmas Flower in North America. The ancient Aztecs prized the poinsettia (cuetlaxochitl in Nahuatl) as a symbol of purity.

In Turkey, it is known as Atatürk's Flower, since it is considered to be the favorite flower of Atatürk, the founder of modern Turkey.

Alternative names for the poinsettia are *Euphorbia pulcherrima*, Mexican Flame Leaf, Christmas Star, Winter Rose, Noche Buena, and Ataturk's Flower (in Turkey). In Nahuatl, one of the major languages spoken in central Mexico, the plant is called *Cuitlaxochitl*, meaning "excrement flower." The name may have come from the observation of birds that would eat the seeds, and then the flowers would appear to germinate from the bird excrement.

Cultivars have been produced with orange, pale green, cream, and marbled leaves.

Poinsettias are shrubs to small trees, typically reaching a height of 0.6 to 4 m (2 to 16 feet). The plant bears dark green dentate leaves that measure 7 to 16 cm (3 to 6 inches) in length. The top leaves, known as bracts, are flaming red, pink, or white and are often mistaken as flowers. The actual flowers are grouped within the small yellow structures found in the center of each leaf bunch, which are called *Cyathea*.

Christmas Delights Cookbook
A Collection of Christmas Recipes
Cookbook Delights Holiday Series Book 12

Caring for Your Poinsettia

Caring for Your Poinsettia

There are exactly 109 varieties of poinsettias available, but 69 percent of Americans still prefer red poinsettias, 7 percent prefer white, and 14 percent prefer pink.

A generally accepted standard is that the plant should be 2½ times taller than the diameter of the container.

Keep your poinsettias at a room temperature between 68 and 70 degrees F. Do not place your plant near cold drafts or excessive heat. Some places to avoid are near appliances, fireplaces, or ventilating ducts.

To protect your poinsettia from chilling winds when transporting plants, carry them in a large shopping bag.

Water thoroughly when the soil feels dry to the touch, but do not let plants sit in standing water. Over watering causes plants to droop.

To keep your plant after the holidays, fertilize after the blooming season with a balanced, all-purpose fertilizer. Do not fertilize when plants are in bloom.

Poinsettias need light, so place them in a bright place for at least six hours a day. In areas outside its natural environment, it is commonly grown as an indoor plant where it prefers good morning sun then shade in the hotter part of the day. However, it is widely grown and very popular in subtropical climates such as Sydney, Australia.

As this is a subtropical plant, it will likely perish if the nighttime temperature falls below 50 degrees F., so it is not suitable for planting in the ground in milder climates. Daytime temperatures in excess of 70 degrees F. tend to shorten the lifespan of the plant.

Your poinsettia can be difficult to induce to reflower after the initial display when purchased. The plant requires a period of uninterrupted long, dark nights for around two months in autumn in order to develop flowers. Incidental light at night during this time will hamper flower production.

Christmas Delights Cookbook
A Collection of Christmas Recipes
Cookbook Delights Holiday Series Book 12

Christmas Facts

Christmas Facts

The Christmas Tree: The tradition of a holiday tree has been around since ancient times and has played an important part in winter celebrations for many centuries. Many pagan festivals used trees to honor gods and spirits. In Northern Europe the Vikings considered the evergreen a symbol and reminder that the darkness and cold of winter would end and the green of spring would return. The Druids of ancient England and France decorated oak trees with fruit and candles to honor their gods of harvests.

In 1841 the English royalty helped popularize the tree in England by decorating the first Christmas tree at Windsor Castle. Prince Albert, husband of Queen Victoria, decorated the first English Christmas Tree with candles, candies, fruits, and gingerbread.

We have taken the Christmas tree from Germany and gift giving from the Dutch tradition of leaving out wooden shoes for them to be filled with goodies. But one tradition remains universal: sharing and caring.

Christmas Colors: The colors most often associated with Christmas decorating are green, red, white, blue, silver, and gold. These colors have been used for centuries and, as with most traditions, the reason may be traced to religious beliefs. In this instance, green represents everlasting life, red represents the bloodline of Jesus Christ, blue represents the sky from which the angels appeared, white represents the purity of the Virgin Birth, and silver and gold represent the richness of God's Blessings.

Christmas Truce in the Midst of World War I: In 1914 there was a truce between German and British troops in France. Soldiers on both sides spontaneously began to sing Christmas carols and stopped fighting. The truce began on Christmas Day and continued for some time afterward. There was even a soccer game between the trench lines in which Germany's 133rd Royal Saxon Regiment is said to have beaten Britain's Seaforth Highlanders 3 to 2.

Christmas Delights Cookbook
A Collection of Christmas Recipes
Cookbook Delights Holiday Series Book 12

Christmas Folklore

Christmas Folklore

Few Americans, to be sure, bother with a Yule log any longer; yet the Yule log was once one of the most firmly entrenched of customs. Often a stump or root, it was brought home Christmas Eve, where it was placed in the kitchen hearth or in the main fireplace. It was lighted with a faggot saved from the year before (lest the house burn down) and kept burning for twelve hours (lest ill luck come). It was not to be bought but was to be obtained from one's own land or from a neighbor's wood, and it had to ignite the first time (lest trouble follow). In some areas the "log" had to be ash, "the ashen faggot," usually a whole tree, cut up, bound, and drawn to the house by oxen. There it was burned, as people told ghost stories and tales of olden times.

There is another story about a war orphan living in an institution who wrote Santa Claus asking that "a real home" be found for him. The orphanage intercepted the letter, publicized it with comments such as "we've just got to find a home or deny the Santa Claus legend." Supposedly, over 100 families responded and were willing to take the child.

Other stories report dying children who have been visited by Santa Claus in September, October, or even June, because they would not live until late December.

More stories tell of hard-bitten soldiers playing Santa to captured enemy youngsters, and of homeless families who appealed to Santa to help them relocate. All testify to the power of our belief that people have an innate right to be visited by Santa Claus and that no effort to protect this right is too great to make. In fact, from 1914 to 1928, when it was investigated unfavorably by the postal authorities, a Santa Claus Association founded by John D. Gluck was not only able to flourish in New York City but was even copied in other towns. Its purpose was to get letters addressed to Santa Claus from the post offices, investigate the circumstances of the children involved, and do for the youngsters whatever was expected.

Christmas Delights Cookbook
A Collection of Christmas Recipes
Cookbook Delights Holiday Series Book 12

Christmas History

Christmas History

The story of Christmas begins with the birth of a baby in Bethlehem. It is believed that Christ was born on the 25th, although the exact month is unknown. It was in 350 A.D. that December 25 was declared the official date for celebrating Christmas by Pope Julius I.

Members of the pagan order have always celebrated the Winter Solstice, the season of the year when days are shortest and nights longest. It was generally believed to be a time of drunkenness, revelry, and debauchery. The pagan Romans called this celebration Saturnalia, in honor of their god Saturn. The festivities began in the middle of December and continued until January 1st. On December 25th, "The Birth of the Unconquerable Sun" was celebrated, as the days gradually lengthened and the sun began to regain its dominance. It is a general pagan belief that the sun dies during the Winter Solstice and then rises from the dead. With cries of "Jo Saturnalia!" the Roman celebration would include masquerades in the streets, magnificent festive banquets, the visiting of friends and the exchange of good-luck gifts known as *Strenae* (lucky fruits). Roman halls would be decked with garlands of laurel and green trees and adorned with lighted candles. Again, as with *Sacaea*, the masters and slaves would exchange places.

Saturnalia was considered a fun and festive time for the Romans, but Christians believed it an abomination to honor such a pagan god. The early converts wanted to maintain the birthday of their Christ Child as a solemn and religious holiday...not one of cheer and merriment, as was the pagan celebration of Saturnalia.

As Christianity spread, however, the church became alarmed by the continuing practice among its flock to indulge in pagan customs and celebrate the festival of Saturnalia. At first, the holy men prohibited this type of revelry, but it was to no avail. Eventually, a decision was made to tame such celebrations and make them into a festive occasion better suited to honor Christ.

Christmas Delights Cookbook
A Collection of Christmas Recipes
Cookbook Delights Holiday Series Book 12

Christmas Symbols

Christmas Symbols

Fir Tree: The pure green color of the stately fir tree remains green all year round, depicting the everlasting hope of mankind. All the needles point toward heaven, making it a symbol of man's thoughts turning toward heaven.

The Star: The star was the heavenly sign of promises long ago. God promised a Savior for the world, and the star was the sign of fulfillment of His promise.

Candle: The candle symbolizes that Christ is the light of the world, and when we see this great light we are reminded of He who displaces the darkness.

Wreath: The wreath symbolizes the real nature of love. Real love never ceases. Love is one continuous round of affection.

Santa Claus: Santa Claus symbolizes the generosity and good will we feel during the month of December.

Holly Leaf: The holly plant represents immortality and the crown of thorns worn by our Savior. The red holly berries represent the blood shed by Him.

The Gift: God so loved the world that He gave His only begotten Son. Thanks be to God for his unspeakable gift.

Wise Men: The wise men bowed before the Holy Babe and presented Him with gold, frankincense, and myrrh. We should always give gifts in the same spirit of the wise men.

Candy Cane: The candy cane represents the shepherds' crook. The crook on the staff helps to bring back strayed sheep to the flock. The candy cane is the symbol that we are our brother's keeper.

Angels: The angels heralded the glorious news of the Savior's birth. The angels sang glory to God in the highest, on earth peace and good will toward men.

Bell: The lost sheep are found by the sound of the bell; it should ring mankind to the fold. The bell symbolizes guidance and return.

Christmas Delights Cookbook
A Collection of Christmas Recipes
Cookbook Delights Holiday Series Book 12

Christmas around the World

Christmas around the World

Germany: Many Christmas practices originate in Germanic countries, including the Christmas tree, the Christmas ham, the Yule log, holly, mistletoe, and the giving of presents.

Australia's Bondi Beach: In the southern hemisphere, Christmas is during the summer. This clashes with the traditional winter iconography, resulting in oddities such as a red fur-coated Santa Claus surfing in for a turkey barbecue.

Japan has adopted Santa Claus for its secular Christmas celebration, but New Year's Day is a far more important holiday.

In India, Christmas is often called bada din ("the big day"), and celebration revolves around Santa Claus and shopping.

In South Korea, Christmas is celebrated as an official holiday.

In The Netherlands, Germany, Scandinavia, Poland, and Lithuania, Christmas Day and the following day are called First and Second Christmas Day.

In Finland, Ireland, Italy, Romania, Austria, and Catalonia (Spain), the day after Christmas is known as St. Stephen's Day.

In Australia, Britain, New Zealand, and Canada December 26th is a holiday. Boxing Day began in England, in the middle of the nineteenth century, under Queen Victoria. Also known as St. Stephen's Day, it was a way for the upper class to give gifts of cash, or other goods, to those of the lower classes.

Several Latin American countries (such as Venezuela) believe that while Santa makes the toys, he then gives them to the Baby Jesus, who is the one who actually delivers them to the children's homes.

In many countries, children leave empty containers for Santa to fill with small gifts such as toys, candy, or fruit.

Children in some countries put their empty shoes out for Santa to fill on the night before Christmas.

Poetry

A Collection of Poetry with Christmas Themes

Table of Contents

Page

Merry Christmas!

The air is cool, the season is snow.
Soon Christmas will come to us who know.
The elves are running for things to do.
In fact, these elves brought this to you!

"Merry Christmas" is a treasure from the Christmas hour
Just leave it up and watch its power.
In your house is where it works,
It cheers up those who stand and lurk.

These yummy treats are for your pleasure,
We've even included a little treasure.
Make two copies to give your friends
They'll have warm fuzzies that never end.

We'll all have a smile upon our face
No one will know who "Merry Christmas'd" this place.
Just one short day, your spell to cast
Or a big snowball will strike you fast!

And don't forget a nifty treat
Like something cute or something sweet.
Please join the fun, let's really hear it.
And spread some Merry Christmas and Christmas Spirit!

Directions:
- Enjoy treats!
- Leave the "Merry Christmas" on your front door.
- Now you have 24 hours to copy this twice, make the Christmas signs and two treat bags…
- Deliver them to two neighbors who don't have a "Merry Christmas" sign.
- Watch how far it goes!

Karen Jean Matsko Hood ©2014
Published in *Christmas Delights Cookbook,* 2014
By Whispering Pine Press International, Inc., 2014

Christmas Eve

Twinkle of night stars
      bring hope

To souls each day
      in prayer.

Spirits rest under morning noon
      in darkness

Peace of night brings gentle breeze,
      in praise

As the sun rises and
      calls all to stand

      Rejoice
        in Christmas light.

Karen Jean Matsko Hood ©2014
Published in *Christmas Delights Cookbook,* 2014
By Whispering Pine Press International, Inc., 2014

Golden Bows

Maple leaves twirl
Circling tendrils on a stem
Suddenly drop and lay still.

Golden bows on boxes
Foil wraps stars that twinkle
Christmas will soon be here.

Will we mail the cards
And wrap the gifts
Place the presents safe?

Remember it is the season
To remember the reason
And why golden bows exist.

Karen Jean Matsko Hood ©2014
Published in *Christmas Delights Cookbook,* 2014
By Whispering Pine Press International, Inc., 2014

Christmas Cactus

Bright pink blossoms unfurl
Painted with fluted edges,
Enthusiastically open to sing
Beautiful melodies bold.
Vivid fuchsia blooms and flames
As they hang in ones and twos,
Artistic advent silhouettes
Against craggy, scalloped frames.

Christmas cactus stems,
Succulent and old,
Shrivel in spots like granny's face
Yet shout the youth of green.

Blossoms of antique lace distend
With morning sunshine.
Birth of the season, chortling delight,
Friendly with tenderness.

Christmas cactus foliage
Lines my way,
Liver-spotted, yet
Bright and young.

Karen Jean Matsko Hood ©2014
Published in *Christmas Delights Cookbook,* 2014
By Whispering Pine Press International, Inc., 2014

Christmas Sweets

Sugar crystals sparkle on an antique silver spoon.
Mom selects brown sugar, white sugar,
confectioner's sugar, crystals, and more.
Granules sparkle white as snow.
Sugar with sweetness that entices your tongue.
Decorations garnish plum fairies,
that dance in your head.
Sugar coats the bristles of paint brushes
as the hand embellishes the palette of old.
Color enlivens his canvas with this
glint of sweetness as he wipes away
his tears of pain. Christmas toys lay
blanketed in white as elves
scurry under the tree.
Visions of fairies that
tiptoe on gossamer wings,
memories of kings
that run by queens.
Christmas dreams.

Karen Jean Matsko Hood ©2014
Published in *Christmas Delights Cookbook,* 2014
By Whispering Pine Press International, Inc., 2014

Shipping Season Continues

Packages ship throughout the year:
Small ones, big ones, short ones, fat ones.
Don't forget the red seal;
bind them up with fiberglass tape.
They cannot break.

Foster child Susie goes to 42nd street;
bundle her up and send her ground.
Air expenses would cost the state
far too much, so "ground" she goes.

Pick up foster child Johnny
from 32nd and drop him in the large box.
Billy goes to 53rd via parcel post;
don't forget the bubble wrap.

Across the conveyor belt he goes,
carefully down the chute.
Oh, a call for a group of siblings
arrives. Can they ship all three?

No box on hand stands tall enough
To pack the trio today.
The state says we must ship right now,
so separate the three we must.

Sibling O, we'll put in box size R;
sibling P we'll stuff in box size H,
sibling A just barely fits in box N.
Hurry, we must get them on their way.

Out the door they go.
Shipping master worries:
What if they get damaged?
Who will pay the price?

Karen Jean Matsko Hood ©2014
Published in *Christmas Delights Cookbook,* 2014
By Whispering Pine Press International, Inc., 2014

Candle Flicker

Sweet beeswax of Christmas candles trickle,
as the fluid flame polishes still.

Darkness smothers the flicker;
it can curl no more.

Dreams of life spiral from the
sleepiness of mind,

In wait of the Christmas star
specks of dust escape all time,

Water condenses on the windowpane,
and seeps down to warp the sill.

Mildew in the tiniest crevices
punctuates the air with the smell of discord.

Ink pen in hand and blank paper,
mellow tacit evening moments.

Christmas glow
and thoughtful memories.

Karen Jean Matsko Hood ©2014
Published in *Christmas Delights Cookbook,* 2014
By Whispering Pine Press International, Inc., 2014

God Sent Children

Gifts in bundles that run on little legs
with mismatched socks and scraped knees;

Packages of chubby voices
bundled in throats that scream with glee;

Some with pigtails and freckled noses,
others in crew cuts and fair skin.

Brilliant as the crimson cardinal on a snowy branch,
Loving as the caress of wind on a winter day.

Thank you for the gifts
in jolly packages with calico faces.

Christmas gifts of children
Winter love.

Karen Jean Matsko Hood ©2014
Published in *Christmas Delights Cookbook,* 2014
By Whispering Pine Press International, Inc., 2014

Christmas Walk Within

Do we really live in the spirit
Ever, sometimes, never?

Or do we only live
in the flesh

Always, usually, often?
How can we live better

in faith and love
to nourish

our souls?
When can we develop

a sense of reality
While a spirit walks

On clouds instead of
within our hearts?

Can we call for
the return of grace?

This Christmas
...or do we have to wait?

Karen Jean Matsko Hood ©2014
Published in *Christmas Delights Cookbook,* 2014
By Whispering Pine Press International, Inc., 2014

Christmas Delights Cookbook
A Collection of Christmas Recipes
Cookbook Delights Holiday Series Book 12

Christmas Traditions

Christmas Traditions

Early Christmas trees were often decorated with apples, nuts, cookies, colored popcorn, and candles. The invention of electricity in the early twentieth century and use of electrical Christmas lights helped spread the use of the Christmas tree.

Boxing Day: In English-speaking countries, the day following Christmas Day is called "Boxing Day." This word comes from the custom which started in the Middle Ages around 800 years ago: churches would open their "alms boxe" (boxes in which people had placed gifts of money) and distribute the contents to poor people in the neighborhood on the day after Christmas. The tradition continues today - small gifts are often given to delivery workers such as postal staff and children who deliver newspapers.

The legend of Santa Claus was brought by Dutch settlers to New York in the early eighteenth century. Santa Claus was depicted as a tall, dignified, religious figure riding a white horse through the air. Known as Saint Nicholas in Germany, he was usually accompanied by Black Peter, an elf who punished disobedient children. In North America he eventually developed into a fat, jolly old gentleman who had neither the religious attributes of Saint Nicholas nor the strict disciplinarian character of Black Peter.

Christmas cards: The custom of sending Christmas cards started in Britain in 1840 when the first "Penny Post" public postal deliveries began. As printing methods improved, Christmas cards were produced in large numbers from about 1860. They became even more popular in Britain when a card could be posted in an unsealed envelope for one half-penny - half the price of an ordinary letter.

Stamps are distributed each year by many nations to commemorate Christmas.

Christmas Delights Cookbook
A Collection of Christmas Recipes
Cookbook Delights Holiday Series Book 12

RECIPES

Christmas Delights Cookbook
A Collection of Christmas Recipes
Cookbook Delights Holiday Series Book 12

Appetizers and Dips

Table of Contents

Page

Cranberry Veggie Balls

These are wonderful vegetarian meatballs with a sweet and sour sauce. They are simple to make and they disappear very quickly. Make these for Christmas holiday parties. If you don't have veggie burger patties, you may use textured vegetable protein (TVP), which is available at most health food stores.

Ingredients for veggie balls:

4	eggs, beaten
1	c. cornflake cereal, crushed
⅓	c. chili sauce
1	Tbs. soy sauce
1½	tsp. dried parsley
2	Tbs. dried onion flakes
8	vegetarian burger patties or textured vegetable protein
2	sleeves buttery round crackers (4 oz.), crumbled
1	pkg. cream cheese (8 oz.), softened
1	c. walnuts, chopped
1	can cranberry sauce (16 oz.)
1	c. Russian style salad dressing (recipe below)
1	tsp. brown sugar
1	Tbs. lemon juice

Ingredients for Russian style salad dressing:

1	c. mayonnaise
¼	c. ketchup
1	Tbs. horseradish
1	tsp. onion, grated

Directions for veggie balls:

1. Preheat oven to 350 degrees F.
2. Spray two baking sheets with nonstick cooking spray.

3. In a medium size mixing bowl, combine eggs, cornflake crumbs, chili sauce, soy sauce, parsley flakes, dehydrated onion, vegetable burger, buttery round crackers, cream cheese, and walnuts.
4. Shape into 72 one-inch meatballs.
5. Arrange on prepared baking sheets.
6. Bake 20 to 25 minutes, or until meatballs are cooked through.
7. In large saucepan, combine cranberry sauce, Russian dressing, brown sugar, and lemon juice.
8. Cook, stirring frequently, until cranberry sauce melts.
9. Add meatballs and heat through.
10. Serve with appetizer toothpicks, if desired.

Directions for Russian style salad dressing:

1. In small bowl, combine all ingredients.
2. Store in refrigerator in tightly sealed container.

Artichoke Green Chile Dip

This is delicious and easy to make. It is also a dip that can be mixed ahead of time, refrigerated until needed, then heated quickly in the microwave when you are ready to serve.

Ingredients:

1 c. mayonnaise
1¼ c. Parmesan cheese, freshly grated
1 c. marinated artichoke hearts, chopped
1 can green chilies (4 oz.), chopped
¼ tsp. garlic salt

Directions:

1. In microwave-safe bowl, combine ingredients.
2. Heat in microwave until hot.
3. Serve with chips or Melba toast rounds.

Bacon Cheese Puffs

These are easy to make and so delicious.

Ingredients:

1½ lb. sliced bacon
2¾ c. Cheddar cheese, shredded
3   Tbs. mustard
1   c. mayonnaise
1   lb. pumpernickel party bread, sliced

Directions:

1. Place bacon in a large, deep skillet, and cook over medium-high heat until evenly brown and crisp.
2. Drain, crumble, and set aside.
3. Preheat oven to broil.
4. In medium bowl, combine bacon, cheese, mustard, and mayonnaise. Stir well.
5. Arrange party bread on a baking sheet.
6. Spoon mixture onto each slice of bread.
7. Broil for 5 minutes until bubbly.

Yields: 30 cheese puffs.

Blue Cheese Dip

This is a simple and delicious blue cheese dip.

Ingredients:

½ lb. bacon
1   tsp. garlic, minced
3   pkg. cream cheese (8 oz. ea.), softened
4   oz. blue cheese
¼ c. walnuts or pecans, chopped

Directions:

1. Preheat oven to 350 degrees F.
2. In large skillet, fry chopped bacon until it is almost done. Stir garlic into the skillet.
3. Remove from skillet; drain excess fat.
4. In medium bowl, mix bacon with cream cheese and blue cheese.
5. Transfer the mixture to a casserole dish.
6. Sprinkle nuts over the dip.
7. Bake 30 to 40 minutes.

Yields: 12 servings.

Crunchy Cheese Ball

This is a savory cheese ball that can be made ahead for your special party. Serve with your favorite crackers.

Ingredients:

1 pkg. cream cheese (8 oz.), softened
¼ c. mayonnaise
2 c. cooked ham, ground
2 Tbs. parsley, chopped
1 tsp. onion, minced
¼ tsp. dry mustard
¼ tsp. hot pepper sauce
¾ c. pistachio nuts, chopped

Directions:

1. In medium bowl, beat cream cheese and mayonnaise until smooth.
2. Stir in ham, parsley, onion, mustard, and pepper sauce.
3. Cover and chill several hours.
4. Form mixture into ball; roll in nuts to coat.

Cherry Peanut Appetizer

This is an unusual, spicy, cherry-peanut appetizer, seasoned with cumin for an unexpected flavor treat.

Ingredients:

- 2   c. peanuts, lightly salted
- 1   c. cherries, tart, dried
- 2   Tbs. hot sauce
- 1-2 tsp. canola oil
- ½   tsp. garlic sauce
- ½   tsp. seasoned salt, or to taste
- ½   tsp. ground cumin
- ¼   tsp. ground red pepper (cayenne pepper), or to taste

Directions:

1. Combine peanuts and cherries in a medium bowl.
2. In small bowl, combine hot sauce, garlic powder, seasoned salt, cumin, and red pepper.
3. Mix well.
4. Pour over peanut mixture, stir to coat.
5. Heat 1 or 2 teaspoons oil in large skillet over medium heat.
6. Add peanut mixture; cook 3 to 4 minutes on medium-high, stirring constantly, until peanuts are light brown.
7. Do not allow mixture to burn.
8. Add more oil if needed.
9. Remove from heat.
10. Spread on parchment paper or aluminum foil to cool.
11. Store in a tightly covered container.

Yields: 3 cups.

Green Olive Spread

This green olive spread is a delicious appetizer for your holiday guests.

Ingredients:

¾   lb. black or green olives, oil-cured
¼-⅓ c. olive oil, plus more for topping
2-3   garlic cloves, minced
½-1   tsp. oregano, dried, crumbled
         pinch of dried rosemary, crumbled
         black pepper to taste, freshly ground
         dash fresh lemon juice
         pinch of hot red pepper flakes (optional)

Directions:

1. Pit olives if not already pit-free.
2. Combine olives, ¼ cup oil, garlic, and herbs.
3. Pulse ingredients together in a blender or food processor to form grainy purée, not a smooth paste.
4. Taste, and add more herbs if necessary, plus black pepper, lemon juice, and hot pepper flakes.
5. Pack mixture into clean jar with airtight lid.
6. Cover the purée with a thin layer of olive oil, then put the lid on and refrigerate.
7. It will keep in refrigerator for a few months.
8. Let come to room temperature before serving.
9. Refrigerate leftovers, adding fresh topping of oil.

Yields: 2 cups.

Did You Know? . . .

Did you know the top Christmas tree producing states are Oregon, North Carolina, Michigan, Pennsylvania, Wisconsin, and Washington?

Hot Dried Beef Spread

This is a delicious, hot appetizer that will disappear quickly.

Ingredients:

1 pkg. cream cheese (8 oz.), room temperature
1 jar dried beef (2½ oz.), shredded
¼ c. red pepper, finely chopped
¼ c. red bell pepper, finely chopped
½ c. onion, finely chopped
½ tsp. black pepper, coarsely ground
½ c. sour cream
¾ c. pecans, chopped

Directions:

1. Preheat oven to 350 degrees F.
2. In large bowl, combine cream cheese well with dried beef, green and red peppers, onion, and black pepper; fold in sour cream.
3. Spoon into casserole dish, and sprinkle chopped pecans over top.
4. Bake 20 minutes.
5. Serve with crackers.

Yields: 8 to 10 servings.

Hot Roasted Chestnuts

There is nothing like the old saying, "Chestnuts roasting on an open fire." Try serving these chestnuts to your family for an appetizer or late night snack. They are delicious.

Ingredients:

large chestnuts, unshelled

Directions:

1. Soak large, unshelled chestnuts in warm water for 30 minutes; drain.
2. With a sharp knife, make a crisscross cut in top of each chestnut.
3. Place all chestnuts in a single layer in foil-lined layer baking pan; sprinkle with salt.
4. Cover pan lightly with foil.
5. Place pan over medium heat and cook gently for 15 minutes.
6. Turn chestnuts and continue cooking, turning occasionally until chestnuts are tender.
7. Let cool slightly before serving.
8. To test chestnuts, open one; inside should be soft.

Raspberry Cheese Ball

This is an easy-to-make cheese ball with holiday red raspberry topping.

Ingredients:

1 pkg. cream cheese (8 oz.), softened
2 Tbs. sherry
¾ c. walnuts or pecans, chopped, toasted
¼ c. seedless raspberry preserves

Directions:

1. In medium bowl, combine cream cheese, sherry, and nuts, mixing until well blended.
2. Chill mixture at least 30 minutes.
3. At serving time, shape into a ball, and then make a hollow on top of ball.
4. Spoon raspberry preserves into hollow and around sides of the ball.
5. Serve with crackers.

Meatballs in Apple Butter

The apple butter and maple syrup give these simple sausage balls a delicious zing.

Ingredients:

    ¾ lb. pork sausage, bulk
    ¼ c. plus 2 Tbs. apple butter
    1 Tbs. maple syrup

Directions:

1. Roll sausage into 1-inch balls. Place on a microwave-safe plate.
2. Cover and microwave on high for 1 to 2 minutes or until a meat thermometer reads 160 degrees F. and meat is no longer pink; drain.
3. Cool; place in a resealable plastic bag.
4. Combine apple butter and syrup, pour over meatballs, and refrigerate overnight.
5. Before serving, transfer meatballs and sauce to a microwave-safe serving dish.
6. Cover and microwave on high for 1 minute or until heated through.
7. Serve immediately.

Nutty O's Snack

Almonds add a nice nutty flavor to this tasty snack. It's perfect for potlucks and not too sweet. Served in a decorative dish, basket, or tin, it has a golden holiday look.

Ingredients:

    1 c. brown sugar, packed
    1 c. dark corn syrup
    ½ c. butter
    12 c. toasted O's cereal
    2 c. pecan halves
    1 c. almonds, whole

Directions:

1. In large saucepan, heat brown sugar, corn syrup, and butter until sugar is dissolved. Stir in cereal and nuts; mix well.
2. Spread onto greased 15 x 10 x 1-inch baking pan.
3. Cool 10 minutes; stir to loosen from pan.
4. Cool completely, and store in an airtight container.

Yields: 21 servings.

Smoked Salmon and Cheese

Salmon and wasabi cream cheese combine to make some delicious appetizers.

Ingredients:

4   oz. cream cheese, softened
1¼ tsp. wasabi powder
2   tsp. lemon juice
1   Tbs. sour cream
4   oz. smoked salmon
10 cucumber slices
    salmon caviar

Directions:

1. In medium bowl, combine cream cheese, Wasabi powder, lemon juice, and sour cream; taste, and adjust seasonings.
2. Spread thin layer of the mixture onto smoked salmon slices, cut in rectangles.
3. Roll up and slice into ¾-inch rounds.
4. Place each round on a peeled cucumber slice, and if desired, garnish top with salmon caviar.
5. For easier slicing, wrap rolls in plastic wrap and freeze 1 hour before cutting.

Yields: 20 bites.

Oysters Rockefeller

This is for fresh oysters on the half shell and is an excellent appetizer for your holiday gathering.

Ingredients:

24 oysters on the half shell
1 c. butter
⅓ c. parsley, finely chopped
¼ c. celery, finely chopped
¼ c. shallots or scallions, finely chopped
½ sm. garlic clove, finely minced
2 c. watercress, chopped
⅓ c. fennel, chopped
⅓ c. bread crumbs, fine, soft
¼ c. anisette or Pernod
    salt and freshly ground black pepper, to taste

Directions:

1. Preheat oven to 450 degrees F.
2. Fill 4 tin pie plates with rock salt.
3. Arrange 6 oysters on each.
4. In a skillet heat the butter, add parsley, celery, shallots, and garlic, and cook 3 minutes.
5. Add watercress and fennel and cook until the watercress wilts, about 1 minute.
6. Pour mixture into an electric blender and add the remaining ingredients.
7. Blend until the sauce is thoroughly puréed.
8. Place 1 tablespoon of sauce on each oyster and spread to the rim of the shell.
9. Bake the oysters just until the sauce bubbles, about 4 minutes.

Yield: 4 servings.

Sesame Chicken Wings

Our family loves chicken wings, and these are very good.

Ingredients:

3   lb. chicken wings (2-2½ doz.)
1   c. butter
1½ c. flour, sifted
6   Tbs. sesame seeds
2   tsp. salt
½ tsp. ground ginger

Directions:

1. Preheat oven to 350 degrees F.
2. Cut off and discard chicken wing tips.
3. Cut each wing in half at the joint, wash, and pat dry.
4. Melt butter in large, shallow baking pan or roasting pan.
5. Combine flour, sesame seeds, salt, and ginger in pie plate.
6. Roll chicken wing pieces in butter, one at a time, letting excess drip off.
7. Roll each wing piece in sesame seed mixture, coating well.
8. Set on wax paper until all are coated.
9. Arrange wings in a single layer in the same baking pan in the remaining butter.
10. Bake 1 hour, or until tender and nicely browned on the bottom.
11. Heat broiler.
12. Broil 5 minutes to brown tops.

Yields: 48 pieces.

Shrimp Cocktail

Once again, this is one of my favorite appetizers. My mom used to make these with canned shrimp when I was young for my birthday treat, and I loved it. This shrimp cocktail sauce is excellent. Be sure and select the freshest shrimp you can.

Ingredients:

- 1 pt. chili sauce, or ketchup if you prefer
- 2 oz. prepared horseradish
- ½ tsp. white pepper
- ½ tsp. salt
- ¼ tsp. dry mustard
- 1 Tbs. hot sauce
- ½ c. celery, chopped
- ½ c. onion, finely chopped
- 1 lb. shrimp in shell (16-20 size)
- 2 Tbs. salt
- 1 gal. water
- 1 lemon, cut in half
  - juice of ½ lemon
  - lemon wedges, cut from remaining ½ lemon
  - fresh lettuce leaves, or shredded lettuce

Directions:

1. In large bowl, combine first 8 ingredients; blend well.
2. Place water, salt, and lemon juice in large pot; bring to boil.
3. Add shrimp and cook 3 to 5 minutes.
4. Drain; chill under cold running water.
5. Peel and devein shrimp.
6. On individual serving plates, arrange shrimp on fresh lettuce leaves or shredded lettuce.
7. Add cocktail sauce, and serve with wedges of fresh lemon.

Christmas Delights Cookbook
A Collection of Christmas Recipes
Cookbook Delights Holiday Series Book 12

Beverages

Table of Contents

Page

Boysenberry Truffle Latte

Boysenberry truffles and coffee make a great holiday drink.

Ingredients:

> 6 oz. hot coffee
> 2 Tbs. chocolate syrup
> 2 Tbs. boysenberry syrup
> 4 oz. chocolate ice cream, or coffee ice cream
> whipped cream
> chocolate, grated
> fresh boysenberries (optional)
> fresh mint leaves (optional)

Directions:

1. Combine coffee, chocolate, and boysenberry syrups in coffee mug.
2. Spoon ice cream into coffee mixture.
3. Top with a dollop of sweetened whipped cream and a sprinkle of grated chocolate.
4. Garnish with boysenberries and mint if desired.

Chai Tea

I always enjoy chai tea, and this makes a wonderful and delicious beverage for all to enjoy.

Ingredients:

> 2 c. water
> 3 Darjeeling blend tea bags
> 1 fresh gingerroot, sliced in 1½-inch strips
> 1 cinnamon stick (2-inch)
> 4 whole cloves
> 1 heaping demitasse spoon powdered cardamom
> 1 vanilla bean (6-inch), cut into 1-inch pieces

1 dash nutmeg
1 Tbs. sugar
¼ c. honey
2 c. milk

Directions:

1. In medium saucepan, bring water to boil; add teabags, ginger, cinnamon stick, cloves, cardamom, nutmeg, and vanilla bean pieces, stirring well.
2. Stir in sugar and honey; reduce heat to simmer.
3. Cook 5 minutes longer, stirring occasionally.
4. Add milk, bring back to boil, and remove from heat.
5. Strain through strainer or coffee filters, and serve hot or in a tall glass filled with ice.
6. Refrigerate unused portion.
7. To reheat, you may either heat any conventional way, or froth with cappuccino maker.

Cranberry-Raspberry Punch

This makes a festive, colorful punch to serve on Christmas Day.

Ingredients:

2 qt. raspberry sherbet
1½ qt. vanilla ice cream
1 qt. cranberry cocktail
1 qt. lemon lime soda

Directions:

1. Soften sherbet and ice cream.
2. In large bowl, combine sherbet, ice cream, and 1 cup of cranberry juice; mix.
3. Add remaining juice; blend well.
4. Just before serving, add lemon lime soda.

Citrus Raspberry Mimosas

My daughter enjoys occasional mimosas, and this is a good one.

Ingredients:

> 6 oz. frozen orange juice concentrate
> 6 oz. frozen pineapple juice concentrate
> 2 c. raspberry juice
> 1 can lemon lime soda (12 oz.), chilled
> orange slices, for garnish
> raspberries, for garnish

Directions:

1. In pitcher or punch bowl, combine orange, pineapple, and raspberry juices.
2. Just before serving, add soda, orange slices, and raspberries.

Yields: 4 servings.

Creamy Raspberry Punch

Try this creamy raspberry punch for your next party gathering.

Ingredients:

> 4 c. apple-raspberry juice, chilled
> 1 c. sparkling water, chilled
> 1 c. milk
> 1 pt. raspberry sherbet
> 1 pt. vanilla ice cream
> 8 oz. frozen raspberries

Directions:

1. In large bowl or pitcher, combine apple-raspberry juice, sparkling water, and milk.
2. Scoop sherbet and ice cream into a large punch bowl.
3. Pour apple-raspberry liquid over top.
4. Garnish with frozen raspberries.

Yields: 10 servings.

Creamy Raspberry Sipper

This recipe makes a refreshing cold drink. Some people do not like raspberry seeds and strain them out. We do enjoy the seeds, and we leave them in the drink.

Ingredients:

1¼ c. fresh raspberries
1¼ c. white grape juice, unsweetened
1½ c. raspberry sherbet
¼ c. water
1 Tbs. lemon juice
10 ice cubes
fresh mint sprigs

Directions:

1. Combine raspberries and grape juice in electric blender, cover, and process until smooth.
2. Combine sherbet, water, and lemon juice in blender container, cover, and process until smooth.
3. Add ice cubes; process until frothy.
4. Garnish with fresh mint sprigs.

Yields: 6 servings.

Egg Safety

Current estimates show there is a 1 in 10,000 chance that the uncooked eggs in your eggnog could contain harmful bacteria. Various egg substitutions have since been found, including a process in which you can now pasteurize your eggs by slowly heating them to 160 degrees F. before using them. Another safe option you can use is to purchase eggnog made in dairies that has already been pasteurized, which means that harmful bacteria have already been eliminated through a heating process.

When you whip up a batch of eggnog, play it safe. Either heat your eggs, or buy the pasteurized eggnog from a dairy and add your own finishing touches. Or, using one more option, try this eggless eggnog recipe.

No Alcohol, Eggless Eggnog

Any who have cooked and prepared food for people with allergies know there is always more than one way to prepare anything. When my children were in preschool, I just asked for a list of what was being prepared that week for lunches and snacks, then made them without the ingredients that caused the allergic reactions. That solved the problem for the other parents in preparing the snacks, and solved major problems for my children.

Ingredients:

    4 c. milk
    1 pkg. French Vanilla instant pudding (3 oz.)
    ½ c. sugar
    4 c. whipping cream
    1 tsp. vanilla extract
    1 tsp. molasses
    1 tsp. rum extract flavoring
    ½ tsp. almond extract flavoring
    1 tsp. nutmeg

Directions:

1. In large bowl, mix the pudding with 1 cup milk.
2. When pudding is setting up, whip cream until thick, adding ½ cup sugar.
3. Add all remaining ingredients, and mix very well.
4. Pour eggnog into festive holiday mugs, and garnish with additional nutmeg.

Yields: 12 servings.

Festive Cherry Punch

Your guests will love this party beverage.

Ingredients:

4 c. cherry juice, blended, chilled
1 liter lemon lime soda, chilled
  ice ring

Directions:

1. Place a ring mold or other decorative mold in freezer, let chill.
2. Rinse the inside of mold with cold water, return to freezer until thin coating of ice forms.
3. Cover bottom of the mold in a decorative pattern with maraschino cherries.
4. Gently add enough cherry juice to cover fruit.
5. Freeze until firm.
6. Gently add more cherry juice blend to fill mold completely. Freeze overnight, or until firm.
7. Just before serving, combine cherry juice blend and lemon lime soda in a large punch bowl.
8. Add ice ring.

Easy Strawberry Frappe

This makes a delicious, refreshing drink using a hand wand blender. You can easily double or triple the recipe and put it in a traditional blender.

Ingredients:

> 1 tsp. sugar or honey
> strawberries
> milk

Directions:

1. Half fill a tall glass with fresh, washed, and sliced strawberries.
2. Add milk, just enough to cover berries.
3. Add sugar.
4. Blend in glass with wand-type hand blender, on fairly high speed, until all lumps are gone and glass has filled up.
5. Serve immediately.

Yields: 1 serving.

Hot Cocoa for Twelve

Try this hot cocoa for a tasty beverage. Serve with marshmallows or a dollop of whipped cream.

Ingredients:

> ½ c. cocoa
> ½ c. sugar
> 3 c. water, divided
> 1 Tbs. vanilla extract
> 1 qt. of evaporated milk or half-and-half cream
>   whipped cream or marshmallows, for garnish

Directions:

1. In a saucepan, blend cocoa and sugar.
2. Gradually stir in ½ cup water and vanilla to make a smooth paste.
3. Add remaining water, bring to boil, and simmer 10 minutes.
4. Meanwhile, scald evaporated milk or half and half over low heat; stir in cocoa mixture.
5. Cover and let stand over lowest heat, and simmer stirring occasionally for 30 minutes to mellow.
6. Pour into mugs and top each serving with marshmallows or whipped cream, if desired.

Hot Spiced Cider

Hot spiced cider fills your home with a magnificent spicy aroma. It is great to have warm on the stove when the kids come in from playing. This is also an inviting drink to welcome guests during the Christmas holidays.

Ingredients:

12 c. apple cider
1 tsp. whole cloves
½ tsp. ground nutmeg
4 sticks cinnamon

Directions:

1. In 3-quart saucepan, over medium-high heat, add cider, cloves, nutmeg, and cinnamon sticks.
2. Heat just to boil; reduce heat to simmer.
3. Simmer uncovered for 10 minutes.
4. Strain cider mixture to remove the spices so the cider does not become too strong in taste.
5. Pour into heated mugs.
6. Serve while hot.

Raspberry Apple Tea

This is a flavorful tea that is refreshing and different from the usual tea.

Ingredients:

    1½ c. raspberry flavored herb tea
    ½ c. apple juice
    ½ c. carbonated water
       sugar, to taste (optional)
       raspberries and apple slices, for garnish
       ice cubes

Directions:

1. In large measuring cup, mix tea and juice together, and pour over ice in 2 tall glasses.
2. Add carbonated water and sugar, if desired.
3. Garnish with fresh raspberries and slices of apple.

Yields: 2 servings.

Raspberry Chocolate Cream Coffee

Your guests will enjoy this drink in front of a fire on a cold winter's eve.

Ingredients:

    ¼ c. heavy cream
    2 Tbs. raspberry syrup
    1 Tbs. chocolate syrup
    1 c. coffee
       ground cinnamon, for garnish
       grated orange peel, for garnish

Directions:

1. In small bowl, whip all but 1 tablespoon of cream.
2. In small saucepan, over low heat, stir reserved tablespoon of cream and raspberry syrup until mixed.
3. Add coffee gradually, stirring constantly.
4. Pour into a mug, and top with whipped cream, cinnamon, and grated orange peel.

Yields: 1 serving.

Raspberry Zinger

Citrus juice adds a refreshing flavor combination to this drink.

Ingredients:

4 c. raspberries, fresh or frozen
½ c. sugar
1 c. orange juice
4 c. vanilla ice cream
2 c. ice, crushed
    whole berries, for garnish

Directions:

1. Purée berries and strain through a fine sieve to yield approximately 2 cups purée.
2. If berries are frozen, partially thaw before puréeing.
3. Combine purée with remaining ingredients.
4. Blend until smooth.
5. Pour into chilled glasses.
6. Garnish with 2 or 3 berries.

Yields: 6 servings.

Strawberry Fruit Shake

This is an easy-to-make fruit shake. Enjoy the wonderful flavors.

Ingredients:

> 1½ c. frozen strawberries, partially thawed
> 1   c. plain yogurt
> ½   tsp. vanilla extract
> 4   Tbs. frozen pineapple concentrate
>   orange or pineapple juice, as needed
>   fresh strawberries, sliced, for garnish

Directions:

1. In blender or food processor, place strawberries, yogurt, vanilla, and frozen concentrate..
2. While blending, add sufficient juice to ingredients so that it will blend to a smooth consistency.
3. Blend quickly.
4. Stop blender once to push berries down with spoon.
5. Serve immediately in chilled glasses.
6. Garnish with fresh sliced strawberries, if desired.

Yields: 2 servings.

Coffee for a Crowd

When you have a large crowd that is too big for your coffee maker, this is a simple solution for making coffee.

Ingredients:

> 1 lb. regular grind coffee
> 3 gal. water

Directions:

1. Place coffee in a clean bag large enough to hold twice that amount to allow for swelling of the grounds and circulation for water.
2. Tie with a strong cord.
3. Measure 3 gallons cold water into large kettle.
4. Heat to full rolling boil, drop in coffee bag, cover.
5. At once turn heat so low that coffee will steep without boiling.
6. Stir several times.
7. Steep 7 to 10 minutes, test for strength.
8. When desired strength has been reached, remove coffee bag, cover.
9. Serve as soon as possible.
10. Do not let the coffee boil at any time.

Yields: 50 cups.

White Zin Raspberry Fooler

This is a non-alcoholic beverage to serve for those who enjoy daiquiri-style drinks without the alcohol.

Ingredients:

4   oz. non-alcoholic white zinfandel
1   oz. raspberry daiquiri mix
2½ oz. lemon lime soft drink
½   oz. grenadine
1   tsp. sugar

Directions:

1. Combine all ingredients.
2. Stir and serve with a smile.

Raspberry-Cider Punch

This is a tasty, clear punch to enjoy.

Ingredients:

5 oz. raspberries, frozen
4 c. sparkling apple cider, chilled
1 Tbs. lime juice

Directions:

1. Purée raspberries; strain through sieve to remove seeds.
2. Combine raspberry purée, apple cider, and lime juice in a pitcher and serve.

Yields: 6 servings.

Hot Lemonade

There is nothing like fresh-squeezed lemonade. This is very good served ice cold with mint leaves. It is also great served warm or hot to sooth a sore throat.

Ingredients:

6 c. water
2 c. lemon juice (about 4 lemons)
1 c. sugar
    lemon or orange slices, for garnish
    fresh mint leaves, for garnish

Directions:

1. Mix water, lemon juice, and sugar until sugar is dissolved.
2. Heat in microwave oven and serve hot.
3. Garnish with lemon slices and mint.

Christmas Delights Cookbook
A Collection of Christmas Recipes
Cookbook Delights Holiday Series Book 12

Breads and Rolls

Table of Contents

A Basic Roll Recipe

This can be used in so many ways that it is good to double the recipe as long as you are making it. The caramel rolls are delicious.

Ingredients for rolls:

1½ c. milk
2   pkg. yeast
½   c. water, lukewarm
2   tsp. salt
½   c. sugar
2   eggs, beaten
½   c. shortening
7-8 c. flour

Additional ingredients for cinnamon roll filling:

¼   c. butter
¼   c. sugar and cinnamon
    powdered sugar, for frosting

Additional ingredients for caramel rolls:

1   c. brown sugar
2   Tbs. corn syrup
3-4 Tbs. water
½   c. walnuts or pecans, chopped
    butter
    cinnamon

Directions for rolls:

1. Heat milk to scalding; cool to lukewarm.
2. Dissolve yeast in lukewarm water.
3. In large bowl, add milk, yeast mixture, salt, sugar, and eggs; mix well.
4. Add about 2 cups of the flour; mix well.
5. Add shortening, then remaining flour.
6. Turn onto a floured surface; knead until smooth.
7. Place in a greased bowl, cover, and let rise 1½ hours, or until double in bulk.
8. Form into parker house, crescent, cloverleaf, or dinner rolls.
9. Place in greased pan, and let rise until double.
10. Bake at 375 degrees F. for 12 to 15 minutes.

11. For hamburger buns, form dough into large buns, 3 inches in diameter, and place them two inches apart on a greased baking sheet.
12. For Coney buns, shape into oblongs.

Yields: 18 rolls.

Directions for cinnamon rolls:

1. After dough has risen the first time, divide into 2 portions and roll out each half on a floured surface.
2. Spread with soft butter and sprinkle with sugar and cinnamon.
3. Add raisins and walnuts, if desired.
4. Roll up and cut in 1-inch slices.
5. Place cut side down on a greased baking sheet or oblong pan.
6. Let rise and bake as above.
7. When partly cool, frost with powdered sugar frosting.

Directions for caramel rolls:

1. In the bottom of a 9 x 13-inch baking pan, combine brown sugar, corn syrup, water, chopped walnuts or pecans, and several small pieces of butter..
2. Place cinnamon rolls, cut side down, in syrup mixture.
3. Continue as for cinnamon rolls.
4. When rolls are done baking, turn out of pan immediately.

Directions for donuts:

1. After dough has risen the first time, punch it down and roll it out on floured surface to ½-inch thick.
2. Cut with a doughnut center.
3. Let rise about halfway, 20 to 30 minutes, and then fry in hot oil, being careful not to burn yourself.
4. Roll doughnuts in sugar.

Directions for maple bars:

1. Roll out dough as for doughnuts.
2. Cut in oblongs 1½-inch wide by 4½-inches long.
3. Fry the same as doughnuts.
4. Frost with maple flavored powdered sugar frosting.

Apple Banana Bread

This is a great combination of flavors. Bananas offer a moist richness, and with the addition of apples, it is really a great snack or served with a meal.

Ingredients:

½ c. butter, softened
½ c. brown sugar
½ c. sugar
2 extra lg. eggs
3 Tbs. sour cream
1 extra lg. banana, mashed
1½ tsp. vanilla extract
1 tsp. baking powder
1 tsp. baking soda
2 c. flour
¾ tsp. cinnamon
2 extra lg. apples, cored, chopped
1 c. walnuts, chopped

Directions:

1. Preheat oven to 350 degrees F.
2. Lightly grease a large loaf pan.
3. In large bowl, cream butter and sugars; beat in eggs.
4. Stir in sour cream, banana, and vanilla.
5. In medium bowl, sift flour, baking powder, baking soda, and cinnamon together.
6. Gradually add to butter mixture.
7. Gently fold in apples and nuts.
8. Spoon into prepared loaf pan.
9. Bake 1 hour, or until inserted toothpick in center comes out clean.
10. Remove from oven and let stand 10 minutes.
11. Turn out onto wire rack to cool.
12. When completely cooled, slice to serve.

Cranberry Chocolate Chip Bread

Cranberries and chocolate combined make great tasting homemade bread. You may want to double the recipe and keep one loaf in the freezer.

Ingredients:

- 1   c. semi-sweet chocolate chips
- 1   c. cranberries, fresh or frozen, coarsely chopped
- ½   c. pecans, chopped
- 2   tsp. orange peel, freshly grated
- 2   c. flour
- 1   c. sugar
- 1½ tsp. baking powder
- ½   tsp. baking soda
- ½   tsp. salt
- 2   Tbs. butter
- ¾   c. orange juice
- 1   egg, slightly beaten

Directions:

1. Preheat oven to 350 degrees F.
2. Grease and flour three 5¾ x 3¼ x 2-inch miniature loaf pans.
3. In small bowl, stir together chocolate chips, cranberries, pecans, and orange peel; set aside.
4. In large bowl, stir together flour, sugar, baking powder, baking soda, and salt.
5. With pastry blender, cut in butter until mixture resembles coarse crumbs.
6. Stir in orange juice, egg, and reserved chocolate chip mixture just until moistened.
7. Divide evenly among prepared pans.
8. Bake 40 to 45 minutes, or until inserted toothpick in center comes out clean.
9. Cool 15 minutes; remove from pans to wire rack.
10. Cool completely, and if desired, drizzle with glaze.

Yields: 3 loaves.

Cherry Candy Cane Twist

This is an attractive and delicious bread, and looks nice served at a buffet or brunch during the holiday season.

Ingredients for bread:

1	pkg. yeast
⅓	c. sugar
⅔	c. water, warm (105-115 degrees F.)
1	c. hazelnuts, toasted, skinned
3	c. flour
1	tsp. salt
¼	c. butter, unsalted, room temperature
1	egg
¾	c. dried cherries

Ingredients for icing:

1½ c. powdered sugar
2-3 Tbs. milk
red food coloring

Directions for bread:

1. Preheat oven to 350 degrees F.
2. Spread hazelnuts on baking sheet.
3. Bake 8 to 10 minutes, or until toasted.
4. Rub nuts in a clean kitchen towel to remove skins.
5. Dissolve yeast and 1 teaspoon sugar in water.
6. Let sit 5 to 10 minutes, or until foamy.
7. Place half the hazelnuts in food processor.
8. Whirl until chopped; remove, and reserve.
9. Place remaining nuts in processor along with remaining sugar; whirl until finely ground.
10. Add flour, salt, and butter to processor.
11. With machine running, add egg and yeast mixture.
12. Whirl until mixture forms a ball.
13. Whirl 30 seconds more to knead.

14. Transfer dough to a large greased bowl.
15. Turn to coat and cover with a damp cloth.
16. Let rise in warm place, away from drafts, 1½ hours, or until double in bulk.
17. Punch dough down.
18. On lightly floured surface, knead in remaining nuts and cherries.
19. Divide dough in half.
20. Roll each half into a 24 inch long rope.
21. Twist ropes together.
22. On a greased sheet, form the twisted loaf into a candy cane shape.
23. Cover with a damp cloth, and let rise in a warm place away from drafts 1 hour, or until double in bulk.
24. Preheat oven to 350 degrees F.
25. Bake for 25 to 30 minutes, or until golden brown and hollow sounding when tapped.
26. Cool bread on wire rack.

Directions for icing:

1. Stir together powdered sugar and milk until mixture is well blended and is of good icing consistency.
2. Divide icing in half.
3. Tint half with red food coloring.
4. Drizzle or pipe red and white icings in candy cane stripes over bread.

Did You Know? . . . .

Did you know there are about 500,000 acres in production for growing Christmas trees in the United States?

Cranberry Date Bread

The red cranberries and dates add flavor, moisture, and especially color to this irresistible bread.

Ingredients:

2⅔ c. powdered sugar, divided
1   c. water
4   c. fresh cranberries
1¾ c. flour, sifted
½   tsp. salt
2   tsp. baking powder
¼   tsp. baking soda
⅓   c. butter, melted
2   eggs, beaten
1   c. walnuts, chopped
1   c. dates, pitted
¼   c. cranberry juice reserved from cooked berries (optional)
2   Tbs. sugar (optional)

Directions:

1. Preheat oven to 350 degrees F.
2. Lightly grease and flour a 9 x 5 x 3-inch loaf pan.
3. In large saucepan, bring 2 cups sugar and water to boil, stirring to dissolve the sugar.
4. Add berries; simmer over low heat for 10 minutes, or until berries pop open.
5. Cool.
6. Drain berries, reserving the juice and measuring 1 cup of berries for use in bread.
7. In medium bowl, sift flour, salt, baking powder, and baking soda together.
8. In large bowl, combine ⅔ cup sugar, butter, eggs, walnuts, dates, and berries.

9. Add flour mixture to the berry mixture, stirring until blended.
10. Pour mixture into prepared loaf pan.
11. Bake 1 hour, or until inserted toothpick in center comes out clean.
12. For a topping (optional): In small saucepan, combine cranberry juice and powdered sugar.
13. Stir over low heat until heated through.
14. Poke a few holes in the baked loaf.
15. Pour on the topping.
16. Cool 10 minutes in the pan.
17. Turn out on a wire rack and cool completely.
18. Wrap in foil and store one day before slicing.

Yields: 1 loaf.

Garlic Bread

Garlic bread is always a welcomed holiday dinner addition.

Ingredients:

2 loaves French bread
1 c. butter, softened
3 garlic cloves, crushed
½ c. Parmesan cheese (optional)

Directions:

1. Preheat broiler.
2. Cut each loaf of French bread in half lengthwise.
3. In small bowl, blend butter, garlic, and Parmesan cheese, if desired.
4. Spread mixture on top of each slice.
5. Place all 4 halves under broiler, butter side up.
6. Broil until buttered tops are golden brown.
7. Slice crosswise into 2-inch pieces, and serve.

Cranberry Orange Loaf

Cranberry and orange make a flavorful bread.

Ingredients:

2   c. flour
1½ tsp. baking powder
½   tsp. baking soda
½   tsp. salt
1   Tbs. orange zest, grated
1½ c. fresh cranberries
1   c. pecans, coarsely chopped
¼   c. butter, softened
1   c. sugar
1   egg
¾   c. orange juice

Directions:

1. Preheat oven to 350 degrees F.
2. Grease and flour a 9 x 5-inch loaf pan.
3. In medium bowl, whisk flour, baking powder, baking soda, and salt together.
4. Stir in orange zest, cranberries, and pecans.
5. Set aside.
6. In large bowl, cream butter, sugar, and egg together until smooth.
7. Stir in orange juice.
8. Beat in flour mixture until just moistened.
9. Pour into prepared pan.
10. Bake 1 hour, or until the bread springs back when lightly touched.
11. Let stand in pan for 10 minutes.
12. Turn out onto a wire rack to cool.
13. Serve.
14. To store, wrap in plastic wrap.

Corn Bread

This is a very tasty corn bread that is always good served hot, right out of the pan. It's wonderful with a hot bowl of chili, and topped off with honey.

Ingredients:

1 pkg. active dry or cake yeast
¼ c. water, very warm
2 c. milk, scalded
⅓ c. sugar
1 c. shortening
1 Tbs. salt
7 c. flour, sifted
2 eggs, well beaten
1 c. yellow cornmeal

Directions:

1. In a measuring cup, sprinkle yeast into very warm water.
2. Stir until dissolved.
3. In large mixing bowl combine milk, sugar, shortening, and salt.
4. Stir in 3 cups of flour, blending well.
5. Stir in eggs, yeast mixture, and cornmeal until well blended.
6. Gradually add and stir in remaining flour.
7. Spoon into a greased 9 x 13-inch baking pan, place in warm area, and let rise slightly.
8. Bake in a preheated oven at 350 degrees F. for 25 to 30 minutes, or until inserted toothpick in center comes out clean.
9. Remove from oven.
10. Cool slightly, and cut into squares.
11. Serve warm with butter.

Focaccia

My family enjoys Focaccia served hot, but its appeal as an Italian flatbread is preserved whether as a side or main dish. The dough is versatile and makes wonderful breadsticks, which are great with a bit of olive oil and grated Parmesan for dipping. Our whole family loves it with pesto.

Ingredients:

    5-6 c. flour (not self rising)
    4   Tbs. fresh or 1 Tbs. dried rosemary leaves, chopped or crumbled
    2   Tbs. sugar
    2   tsp. salt
    2   pkg. active dry yeast
    6   Tbs. olive or canola oil
    2   c. water, very warm (120-130 degrees F.)
    4   Tbs. olive oil
    ¾   c. Parmesan cheese, grated
        canola oil

Directions:

1. In large bowl, combine 2 cups flour, the rosemary, sugar, salt, and yeast.
2. Add 6 tablespoons oil and the warm water.
3. Beat with electric mixer on medium speed 3 minutes, scraping bowl frequently.
4. Stir in enough remaining flour until dough is soft and leaves sides of bowl.
5. Place dough on lightly floured surface.
6. Knead 5 to 8 minutes until dough is smooth and springy.
7. Place dough in large bowl greased with canola oil, turning dough to grease all sides.
8. Cover bowl loosely with plastic wrap; let rise in warm place 30 minutes, or until almost double in bulk.
9. Dough is ready if indentation remains when touched.

10. Grease 2 baking sheets or 12-inch pizza pans with small amount of oil.
11. Gently push fist into dough to deflate; divide dough in half.
12. Shape each half into a flattened, 10-inch round lightly coated with cooking spray.
13. Let rise in warm place 30 minutes, or until double in bulk.
14. Gently make depressions about 2 inches apart in dough with fingers.
15. Carefully brush with 4 tablespoons olive oil.
16. Sprinkle with Parmesan.
17. Bake in preheated oven at 400 degrees F. for 15 to 20 minutes.
18. Remove from oven, and serve warm or cool.

Croutons for Soup or Salad

These croutons are so easy to make and are delicious.

Ingredients:

4-5 slices bread
½ c. olive oil
2 lg. garlic cloves, minced
⅓ c. Parmesan cheese, grated
1-2 Tbs. dry parsley

Directions:

1. Preheat oven to 325 degrees F.
2. In small bowl, combine last 4 ingredients together.
3. Using pastry brush, brush both sides of slices with oil mix. Cut into small squares.
4. Place single layers on baking sheets.
5. Bake 10 to 15 minutes, or until golden.
6. Cool.
7. Keeps in sealed container 4 to 6 weeks.

Poteca Recipe

This is the version of poteca dough that my mom used to make her poteca. She tried other poteca recipes but this was her standard recipe. Each time she would make poteca it would turn out a little different but it was always delicious.

Ingredients for basic poteca dough:

1   c. milk, scalded
1   c. sugar
3   tsp. salt
½ c. butter
1   c. water, warm
4   pkg. active dry yeast or 4 cakes
4   eggs, beaten
10 c. flour, sifted, divided
¼ c. butter, melted
    sprinkle with flour, to prevent sticking to board

Ingredients for poteca filling:

2½ lb. walnuts, ground
2   c. graham crackers, ground
2½ c. sugar
½ c. honey
1   c. butter
1   c. cream
2   tsp. vanilla
½ tsp. lemon juice
4   eggs, beaten

Directions for basic sweet dough:

1. In medium bowl, combine milk, sugar, salt, and butter; mix well. Cool to lukewarm.

2. In large bowl, add water; sprinkle or crumble yeast on top. Stir until dissolved.
3. Stir in milk mixture.
4. Stir in eggs and 6 cups of flour; beat until smooth.
5. Stir in remaining flour; beat until smooth.
6. Turn dough out on lightly floured surface.
7. Knead until smooth and elastic.
8. Place in greased bowl; brush top with butter.
9. Cover; let rise 1 hour in warm place, free from drafts, until double in bulk.
10. Punch down and turn out on lightly floured surface.
11. Proceed to make desired shapes and use for your favorite recipes of poteca or poppy seed filling.
12. Note: For faster sweet dough, use 3 packages or cakes of yeast and it will rise in 45 minutes.
13. Feel free to reduce the ingredients to make a smaller batch.

Directions for filling:

1. In large bowl, combine all ingredients.
2. Melt butter and use a pastry brush to brush on stretched dough.
3. Spread filling on prepared dough.
4. Starting at wide side of dough, roll up as for jellyroll.
5. Seal edges.
6. Gently pull dough to make a 25-inch roll.
7. Form into a snail shape on a large greased baking sheet.
8. Cover; let rise in warm place, free from draft, until double in bulk, about 1 hour.
9. Bake 325 degrees F. 40 to 45 minutes, or until done.
10. Remove from baking sheet; cool on wire rack.
11. Cut in slices.
12. This freezes well. Some prefer to serve it warm, and others enjoy it cold. Either way, it is delicious.

Panetone

If you're looking for a bit different kind of bread, you will love this one from Italy with lemon and golden raisins, baked in a coffee can.

Ingredients:

1	Tbs. yeast
1	c. warm water
1	tsp. salt
½	c. sugar
2	eggs and 2 yolks
1	tsp. vanilla extract
1	lemon, zested, juiced
¼	c. canola oil
4½-5	c. flour
1	c. golden raisins
2	coffee cans (1-lb. size), greased

Directions:

1. Preheat oven to 350 degrees F.
2. In small cup, dissolve yeast in warm water.
3. In medium bowl, combine salt, sugar, eggs, vanilla, lemon rind, and lemon juice.
4. Stir in dissolved yeast; set aside.
5. In large bowl, measure 4 cups flour.
6. Add liquid mixture, stirring well.
7. Stir in raisins.
8. Knead dough 10 to 15 minutes, or until smooth and silky, adding more flour as needed.
9. Place dough in an oiled bowl, cover, set in a warm place, and let rise until double in size.
10. When doubled, place in 2 greased coffee cans.
11. Let rise until doubled again.
12. Bake 35 minutes.

Yields: 2 loaves.

Christmas Delights Cookbook
A Collection of Christmas Recipes
Cookbook Delights Holiday Series Book 12

Breakfasts

Table of Contents

Page

Belgian Waffles with Cherry Sauce

These thick, hearty waffles are a family favorite and are very tasty, served with cherry sauce and whipped cream topping.

Ingredients for cherry sauce:

¼ c. sugar
2   tsp. cornstarch
⅛ tsp. cinnamon
½ c. orange juice
2   c. sweet cherries
1   tsp. orange peel, grated

Ingredients for waffles:

2   c. flour
2   Tbs. sugar
1½ tsp. baking powder
½ tsp. salt
2   c. milk
½ c. butter, melted
4   egg yolks, beaten
4   egg whites, beaten stiff
    sweetened whipped cream

Directions for cherry sauce:

1. In small saucepan, combine sugar, cornstarch, and cinnamon.
2. Add orange juice, cherries, and orange peel; mix well.
3. Place saucepan, over medium-high heat, and bring to a boil.
4. Boil until thickened.
5. Serve over waffles.

Directions for waffles:

1. In large bowl, combine flour, sugar, baking powder, and salt.
2. In small bowl, mix milk, melted butter, and egg yolks; add to dry ingredients, stir just to moisten.
3. Fold in stiffly beaten egg whites.
4. Bake in waffle iron according to manufacturer's instructions.
5. Serve topped with sweetened whipped cream.

Christmas Morning German Pancakes

This is an easy recipe for busy families. Our entire family enjoys this easy-to-make, oven-puff pancake. We occasionally double the recipe and make two pans for dinner. It is good plain or with your favorite syrup, preserves, or berries.

Ingredients:

4   eggs
1¼ c. milk
1   c. flour
½   c. butter

Directions:

1. Preheat oven to 375 degrees F.
2. Slice butter into a 9 x 13-inch baking pan, place in oven.
3. When butter starts to sizzle, remove pan from oven.
4. In blender container, add eggs and milk; blend well.
5. Add flour; blend until smooth.
6. Pour mixture into pan and place pan back into oven.
7. Bake 15 to 20 minutes.
8. Tip out of pan, dust with powdered sugar, and serve hot with butter and your favorite syrup.

Buckwheat Pancakes with Chokecherry Sauce

Between the buckwheat and chokecherries, this is a delicious combination that will satisfy the taste buds of all the family for breakfast.

Ingredients for sauce:

1½ c. chokecherries
¾ c. water, cold
1   box cherry gelatin (3 oz.)
2   Tbs. fresh orange juice
2   Tbs. butter, unsalted
½   tsp. honey

Ingredients for pancakes:

1   c. buckwheat flour
1   c. flour
¼   tsp. salt
3   tsp. baking powder
2   lg. eggs
1½ c. buttermilk
5   tsp. honey
2   Tbs. canola oil
¼   c. seltzer water

Directions for sauce:

1. Place cherries into a medium saucepan and pour water on top.
2. Bring to boil, cover with lid, and reduce heat to low. Let simmer 10 minutes.
3. Reduce heat to lowest setting and stir in dry gelatin, orange juice, butter, and honey, mixing until all is blended well and butter has melted.

4. Turn off heat and leave in pan on top of burner while you continue with the pancakes.
5. Reheat sauce slightly, if necessary, before serving.

Directions for pancakes:

1. In large bowl, combine flours, salt, and baking powder together.
2. In separate bowl, whisk together eggs, buttermilk, honey, and oil.
3. Pour egg mixture into flour mixture and stir gently just to moisten.
4. Carefully add seltzer and mix gently. Do not over mix; batter should be lumpy.
5. Using timer, let batter rest for 10 minutes.
6. While batter is resting, heat lightly greased griddle over medium heat.
7. Ladle out ¼ cup portions of batter onto the hot pan and cook until the edges start to form up and a few bubbles have started to pop on the surface.
8. Flip over using a wide spatula and cook until browned on the bottom. It will only take a few minutes per side.
9. Repeat until all batter has been cooked.
10. Serve pancakes with the chokecherry sauce ladled over the top.

Yields: 10 to 12 pancakes.

Did You Know? . . . .

Did you know our early holiday experiences shape our lifetime expectations of these special occasions? If you begin when your kids are very young to emphasize the religious, cultural, and altruistic traditions of Christmas, and if you de-emphasize the commercial hoopla, you will be giving them gifts that will last far longer than any toys that money can buy.

French Toast with Raspberry Sauce

The cream cheese topping makes yet another variation to your French toast.

Ingredients for French toast:

    1 loaf French bread
    4 eggs
    1 pt. heavy whipping cream
    ¼ tsp. nutmeg
    1 tsp. vanilla extract

Ingredients for sauce:

    1 jar raspberry jam
    ¾ jar orange juice
    2 Tbs. butter

Ingredients for topping:

    1 pkg. cream cheese (8 oz.)
    1 sm. can pineapple
    2 tsp. cream
       nuts, for garnish
       fresh raspberries, for garnish

Directions for French toast:

1. In deep-dish pie plate, combine eggs, whipping cream, nutmeg, and vanilla; dip bread slices in mixture.
2. In large skillet, over medium heat, melt butter.
3. Sauté bread slices until golden on both sides.
4. Note: Centers cook better if the pan is covered.

Directions for sauce:

1. In small saucepan, simmer jam, orange juice, and butter together.

2. Allow sauce to reduce somewhat.
3. Serve warm over the toast slices.

Directions for topping:

1. In blender or food processor, blend cream cheese, pineapple, and cream.
2. Serve on top of sauced French toast.
3. Garnish with nuts, raspberries, and mint sprig.

Huckleberry Fritters

My mom used to make us warm apple fritters for breakfast as a special treat when I was a kid. This is an alternate version and makes a special, easy-to-make breakfast. These are delicious served warm.

Ingredients:

1½ c. flour
¾ c. sugar
3   tsp. baking powder
¾ c. fresh huckleberries
1   egg, beaten
1   c. milk
    canola oil, for frying
    powdered sugar, cinnamon, and sugar (optional)

Directions:

1. In large bowl, sift together dry ingredients; add berries.
2. Mix egg and milk; add to dry mixture.
3. Mix just until moistened.
4. Drop batter by tablespoons into deep hot oil set at 375 degrees F.
5. Fry until golden brown, 3 to 4 minutes, turning once.
6. Drain on paper towel.
7. Roll in powdered sugar, granulated sugar, or cinnamon and sugar.

Ham Stuffed Onion Biscuits

This is a wonderful recipe to use when you are having a special occasion to celebrate. They are delicious for a leisurely breakfast or brunch.

Ingredients for dish:

1 Tbs. butter
½ med. onion, finely diced
1 garlic clove, finely minced
1 lb. cooked ham, diced
1 Tbs. fresh parsley, chopped
1 pinch dried thyme
12 hot biscuits, split in half (recipe below)
   fresh parsley sprigs, for garnish

Ingredients for cheese sauce:

1 c. butter
1 c. flour
1 tsp. salt
½ tsp. pepper
2 qt. milk, cold
¾ c. American or processed cheese, grated

Ingredients for 12 biscuits:

2 c. flour, self-rising
½ tsp. baking soda
¼ tsp. cream of tartar
1 Tbs. sugar
5 Tbs. shortening
1 c. buttermilk

Directions for dish:

1. In a cast iron skillet, sauté onion and garlic in butter until golden brown.

2. Add ham and seasonings; stir in cheese sauce, and keep warm.
3. Arrange open biscuits on serving plates.
4. Place a ladleful of ham and cheese mixture in the center of each biscuit, garnish with parsley sprigs, and serve at once.

Directions for cheese sauce:

1. In small saucepan, melt butter over medium heat.
2. Add flour and continue stirring briskly with wooden spoon until smooth.
3. Add salt and pepper.
4. Gradually stir in cold milk, stirring briskly until all is added.
5. Continue to cook, while stirring, for about 10 minutes; mixture will continue to thicken.
6. Add grated cheese after 10 minutes of cooking, and continue stirring until cheese is melted and sauce is desired thickness.
7. Add to ham mixture in order called for.

Directions for biscuits:

1. Preheat oven to 425 degrees F.
2. In large bowl, whisk flour, baking soda, cream of tartar, and sugar together.
3. Cut in shortening with a pastry cutter or 2 knives.
4. Add buttermilk and stir until mixed well.
5. Place the dough on a well-floured surface and knead 3 times.
6. Pat out the dough and cut with a round biscuit cutter.
7. Re-pat the scraps and cut again.
8. Place biscuits on a baking sheet.
9. Bake 8 to 10 minutes, or until golden brown.
10. Remove from oven and serve hot.

Yields: 6 to 12 servings.

Poppy Seed Roll (Yugoslavian)

Homemade poppy seed filling is rolled inside tender yeast dough and baked until golden brown in this old Yugoslavian treat. My mother and aunts always made this Eastern European bread for Easter and Christmas. Looks complicated but it is worth the extra time it takes to make. Enjoy this delicious poppy seed dessert, which is also served at breakfast. You can use this dough recipe or use the dough recipe included in the Poteca Recipe.

Ingredients for dough:

4 pkg. active dry yeast (.25 oz.)
2 c. water, warm (100 degrees F.)
½ c. sugar
8 c. all-purpose flour or more if needed
1 tsp. salt
¼ c. butter, to spread on dough while stretching
1 egg, separated, white reserved

Ingredients for filling:

2 lb. poppy seeds
1½ c. white sugar
¼ c. butter
2 Tbs. lemon juice
1 c. honey
2 c. milk, hot

Directions for dough:

1. Mix yeast with water and 8 tablespoons sugar in a small bowl. Allow to stand until yeast forms a creamy layer.
2. Whisk flour with salt in a bowl; use a pastry cutter to cut 1 cup butter into flour mixture until mixture resembles coarse crumbs.

102

3. Pour yeast mixture and egg yolk into flour mixture and stir to make a soft dough.
4. Turn dough onto a floured work surface and knead until smooth and slightly springy, about 5 minutes. If dough is too sticky, knead in more flour, about 2 tablespoons at a time.
5. Cut dough into eight equal pieces. Roll each piece out into a 12 × 16-inch rectangle.
6. Spread half the poppy seed filling over each rectangle, leaving a 1-inch border. Fold the 1-inch border back over the filling on all sides and press down.
7. Pick up shorter side of a dough rectangle and roll it like a jellyroll; repeat with second rectangle.
8. Pinch ends together or tuck ends under to prevent filling from leaking out.

Directions for filling:

1. Grind poppy seeds in old-fashioned poppy seed grinder or place poppy seeds into a food processor and process until seeds are ground, about 1 minute.
2. Mix poppy seeds with 1 cup sugar, 4 tablespoons melted butter, lemon juice, 1 cup honey, and hot milk in a bowl; stir to combine.
3. Cover poppy seed filling and refrigerate while making bread (filling will set up and thicken as it chills).

Yields: 2 filled loaves.

Raspberry Breakfast Bars

These breakfast bars are easy to make and so delicious.

Ingredients for crust:

  1 c. flour
  1 c. quick cooking rolled oats
  ⅔ c. brown sugar, packed
  ¼ tsp. ground cinnamon
  ⅛ tsp. baking soda
  ½ c. butter, melted

Ingredients for filling:

  2 c. raspberries, fresh or frozen
  2 Tbs. sugar
  2 Tbs. water
  1 Tbs. lemon juice
  ½ tsp. ground cinnamon

Directions for crust:

  1. Preheat oven to 350 degrees F.
  2. In large bowl, stir flour, oats, brown sugar, ¼ teaspoon cinnamon, and baking soda together.
  3. Stir in melted butter until thoroughly combined.
  4. Set aside 1 cup of oat mixture for topping.
  5. Press remaining oat mixture into an ungreased 9 x 9 x 2-inch baking pan.
  6. Bake 20 to 25 minutes.

Directions for filling:

  1. In medium saucepan, combine berries, sugar, water, lemon juice, and ½ teaspoon cinnamon.
  2. Bring to boil; reduce heat, and simmer uncovered for 8 minutes, or until slightly thickened, stirring frequently. Remove from heat.
  3. When crust is done, remove from oven and carefully spread filling on top of baked crust.

4. Sprinkle with reserved oat mixture, lightly pressing oat mixture into filling.
5. Bake 20 to 25 minutes more, or until topping is set.
6. Cool in pan on wire rack.
7. Cut into bars.

Yields: 18 bars.

Crêpes

This is a favorite of the Hood Family. These crêpes are made frequently for special breakfasts. The good thing about this breakfast is that everyone in your family can assemble their own and add their favorite fruits and toppings.

Ingredients:

   8 lg. eggs
   2 c. milk
   5 Tbs. butter, melted
   2 c. flour, sifted
   1 c. sugar
      assorted fresh fruits or jams and jellies
      powdered sugar (optional)
      whipped cream (optional)

Directions:

1. In blender, mix eggs, milk, butter, flour, and sugar in blender; process until smooth.
2. Pour approximately ½ cup into buttered skillet that has been heated to medium-high heat.
3. When crepe is looking dry and is lightly browned on the bottom, flip to other side and lightly brown.
4. Place on plate and fill with your favorite fresh fruits or jams and jellies.
5. Roll up and sprinkle with powdered sugar.
6. Serve with a dollop of sweetened whipped cream for a delicious breakfast.

Granny Smith Coffee Cake

My daughter especially likes coffee cake, and this is a tasty apple version of the traditional favorite.

Ingredients:

- 1 pkg. cream cheese (8 oz.), softened
- 1½ c. sugar, divided
- ⅓ c. butter
- 2 eggs
- 1 tsp. almond extract
- 1¾ c. flour
- 1 tsp. baking powder
- ½ tsp. baking soda
- ½ tsp. salt
- ¼ c. milk
- 4 c. Granny Smith apples, pared, cored, sliced
- 2 Tbs. lemon juice
- 2 Tbs. flour
- 2 tsp. ground cinnamon

Directions:

1. Preheat oven to 350 degrees F.
2. Lightly grease and flour a 9 x 13-inch baking pan.
3. In large bowl, combine cream cheese, 1 cup sugar, butter, eggs, and almond extract; mix well.
4. In medium bowl, sift flour, baking powder, baking soda, and salt together.
5. Blend into cheese mixture alternately with milk.
6. Pour into prepared baking pan.
7. Dip apples into lemon juice; toss with 2 tablespoons flour, remaining sugar, and cinnamon.
8. Arrange apple slices on coffee cake.
9. Bake 50 to 60 minutes, or until inserted toothpick in center comes out clean.
10. Remove from oven, cool slightly, and then cut into squares to serve warm.

Raspberry Scones

For a truly decadent morning meal try these raspberry scones.

Ingredients:

2 c. flour
½ tsp. salt
2 tsp. baking powder
¼ tsp. baking soda
¼ c. butter
1 c. raspberries
⅔ c. buttermilk
1 Tbs. molasses
   nonstick cooking oil spray

Directions:

1. Preheat oven to 450 degrees F.
2. Lightly spray a baking sheet with cooking oil.
3. In large bowl, combine flour, salt, baking powder, and baking soda; mix well with a fork.
4. Cut in butter with pastry blender or fork until coarse crumbs are formed.
5. In small bowl, combine buttermilk and molasses.
6. Add raspberries and buttermilk mixture to flour mixture; stir well.
7. Turn dough out onto a floured surface.
8. To avoid crushing berries, use hands to pat into ½-inch thickness.
9. Cut into triangles.
10. Arrange on greased baking sheet.
11. Bake 12 minutes, until browned.
12. Serve hot with butter.

Yields: 10 servings.

Raspberry-Fig Breakfast Bar

My daughter and son love fig cookies. This makes an interesting combination of raspberry and figs for a delicious breakfast bar.

Ingredients for fig purée:

1½ c. dried figs, coarsely chopped
1   c. water
2   Tbs. honey

Ingredients for breakfast bar:

4½ c. flour
3   tsp. baking powder
3   c. brown sugar
4½ c. oats
½   c. butter, softened
1½ c. fig purée
8   oz. raspberry jam
    nonstick cooking oil spray

Directions for fig purée:

1. In small saucepan, combine figs, water, and honey.
2. Bring to boil, cover, reduce heat, and simmer 20 minutes until softened.
3. Pour fig mixture into food processor, and purée 10 seconds until smooth.

Directions for breakfast bar:

1. Preheat oven to 250 degrees F.
2. Mix all ingredients except jam; form into crumbs.
3. Press half of mixture into pan sprayed with nonstick oil.
4. Spread jam on crumb crust.
5. Form top layer with remaining mixture.
6. Bake 50 to 60 minutes.

Christmas Delights Cookbook
A Collection of Christmas Recipes
Cookbook Delights Holiday Series Book 12

Cakes

Table of Contents

Page

Caramel Cake

My husband has always enjoyed caramel, and this makes a great-tasting cake.

Ingredients for cake:

    1   c. sugar
    ½   c. water, boiling
    ½   c. butter, softened
    1⅓ c. sugar
    3   eggs
    2⅓ c. flour
    2½ tsp. baking powder
    1   tsp. salt
       water, cold

Ingredients for caramel icing:

    6   Tbs. butter
    ¼   c. caramel mixture (directions below)
    ¼   c. cream
    3   c. powdered sugar, sifted
    ⅓   tsp. salt
    1   tsp. vanilla extract

Directions for caramelizing sugar:

1. Melt sugar in heavy pan over low heat, stirring constantly.
2. Heat until melted to golden brown syrup.
3. Remove from heat.
4. Slowly add ½ cup boiling water to caramelize sugar.
5. Stir constantly over low heat until lumps are dissolved.
6. Pour into measuring cup.
7. Set ¼ cup aside to be used in icing.

8. To remaining ¼ cup, add enough cold water to equal 1 cup of liquid.

Directions for cake:

1. Preheat oven to 350 degrees F.
2. Grease and flour two 9-inch layer pans or a 9 x 13-inch baking pan.
3. In large bowl, cream butter and sugar together.
4. Beat in eggs.
5. In another bowl, sift flour, baking powder, and salt together.
6. Stir into sugar and egg mixture, alternating with caramel mixture.
7. Pour batter into prepared pans.
8. Bake 30 to 35 minutes for layer pans.
9. If using an oblong pan, bake for 35 to 45 minutes.
10. Cool.

Directions for caramel icing:

1. In small saucepan, heat butter, caramel, and cream.
2. Beat in sugar, salt, and vanilla.
3. Spread icing over cooled cake.

Did you Know? . . . .

Did you know that in 1939, an advertising employee at the department store Montgomery Ward wrote the story of Rudolph the Red-Nosed Reindeer for a store promotion? That year the store gave away 2.4 million copies of the story.

Did you Know? . . . .

Ten years later, Gene Autry recorded the song "Rudolph the Red-Nosed Reindeer." Since then it has sold over 80 million copies. Rudolph has definitely gone down in our holiday history.

Cheesecake with Raspberry Sauce

This is a delicious, lighter version of cheesecake. The cottage cheese adds protein and lightens this recipe. The raspberry topping tastes great and looks very festive.

Ingredients for cheesecake:

¼ c. graham cracker crumbs
2 c. cottage cheese, well-drained
18 oz. cream cheese, cut into cubes
1 c. sugar
2 Tbs. cornstarch
1 tsp. vanilla extract
1 egg
2 egg whites

Ingredients for raspberry sauce:

14 oz. frozen raspberries, thawed
1 Tbs. cornstarch
¾ c. raspberry jelly, heated

Directions for cheesecake:

1. Preheat oven to 450 degrees F.
2. Lightly grease 9-inch springform pan; sprinkle graham crumbs evenly over bottom.
3. In blender or food processor, purée cottage cheese until smooth.
4. Add cream cheese; process until smooth.
5. With processor on, gradually add sugar, cornstarch, and vanilla.
6. Add egg and egg whites, one at a time, to cream cheese mixture; process using on and off action until just blended; pour into pan.
7. Bake 10 minutes; reduce heat to 250 degrees F., and bake 35 to 40 minutes.

8. Cool and then refrigerate overnight.
9. Serve with raspberry sauce.

Directions for raspberry sauce:

1. Drain thawed raspberries, reserving juice.
2. Place berries in sieve; crush to extract additional juice. Discard seeds.
3. In microwave-safe bowl, whisk cornstarch and heated jelly into berry juice.
4. In microwave on high, cook 1 to 2 minutes until thickened; refrigerate until cool.

Yields: 1 cheesecake with 1¼ cups sauce.

Old-Fashioned Pound Cake

My husband loves pound cake, and this is an easy to make version.

Ingredients:

1   c. butter
1¾ c. sugar
1   tsp. vanilla extract
4   lg. eggs
2   c. flour

Directions:

1. Preheat oven to 350 degrees F.
2. In large bowl, with electric mixer, cream butter, sugar, and vanilla until fluffy; add eggs, one at a time, beating after each addition.
3. Continue beating on high speed for 10 minutes.
4. Fold in flour; do not beat.
5. Pour into greased and floured tube baking pan.
6. Bake 1 hour.

Chocolate Raspberry Flourless Cake

This is an intense chocolate cake with subtle raspberry flavor.

Ingredients for cake:

> 12 pieces bittersweet (not unsweetened) or semi-sweet
>   chocolate, chopped
> ¾ c. butter, unsalted, cut into pieces
> 6 lg. eggs, separated
> 6 Tbs. sugar
> 6 Tbs. raspberry syrup
> 2 tsp. vanilla extract

Ingredients for glaze:

> ½ c. whipping cream
> ⅓ c. dark corn syrup
> 3 Tbs. raspberry syrup
> 9 oz. bittersweet or semi-sweet chocolate, chopped

Directions for cake:

1. Preheat oven to 350 degrees F.
2. Butter a 9-inch springform pan.
3. Line bottom of pan with parchment or wax paper; butter the paper.
4. Wrap outside of pan with foil to prevent water from seeping in.
5. In heavy, medium saucepan, over low heat, stir chocolate and butter until melted and smooth (or microwave at medium, stirring frequently).
6. Remove from heat.
7. Cool to lukewarm, stirring often.
8. Using electric mixer, beat egg yolks and sugar until very thick and pale, about 3 minutes.

9. Fold lukewarm chocolate mixture into yolk mixture, and then fold in vanilla extract.
10. Using clean, dry beaters, beat egg whites in another large bowl until stiff peaks form.
11. Gradually add 6 tablespoons raspberry syrup until all is incorporated.
12. Fold egg white mixture into chocolate mixture in 3 additions. Pour batter into prepared pan.
13. Bake 45 minutes until top is puffed and cracked, or inserted toothpick in center comes out with a few moist crumbs.
14. Cool cake in pan on rack. Don't worry... the cake will fall.
15. Gently press down on top of cake to make an evenly thick cake.
16. Loosen sides of pan with small knife; remove pan sides.
17. Invert cake onto serving plate and peel off parchment paper.

Directions for glaze:

1. In medium saucepan, bring cream, corn syrup, and raspberry syrup to simmer; remove from heat.
2. Add chocolate; whisk until melted and smooth.
3. Spread ½ cup glaze over top and sides of cake.
4. Freeze 3 minutes, until almost set.
5. Pour additional ½ cup (or remaining glaze for a more intense chocolate flavor) over cake, smooth sides, and then spread on top.
6. Chill 1 hour, until glaze is firm.
7. Serve with a dollop of sweetened whipped cream on top, and garnish with chocolate shavings.

Did you Know? . . . .

Did you know that on Christmas Eve in 2001, the Bethlehem Hotel had 208 of its 210 rooms free?

Christmas Whiskey Cake

This is a really good, light fruitcake. You may substitute orange juice for the whiskey.

Ingredients for cake:

- 1 c. butter
- 2 c. sugar
- 6 lg. eggs
- 3 c. flour, sifted
- 2 tsp. baking powder
- ½ tsp. salt
- 3 c. white raisins (or candied fruit)
- 1 tsp. nutmeg
- 1 lb. pecans, chopped
- 1 c. bourbon

Ingredients for liquid mixture:

- ⅓ c. sugar
- ½ c. whiskey
- ¼ c. water
- 2 Tbs. butter

Directions for cake:

1. Preheat oven to 300 degrees F.
2. Lightly grease and flour a baking pan.
3. In large bowl, beat butter with electric mixer.
4. Add sugar, mix until creamed; add eggs, beat well.
5. In large bowl, sift flour, baking powder, and salt together; add to creamed mixture.
6. Add raisins, nutmeg, pecans, and bourbon.
7. Pour batter into prepared baking pan.
8. Bake 1½ hours, or until golden brown and dry on top. Miniature loaf pans, bake 1 hour.
9. Remove from pan and place on a plate.
10. Place back in pan and poke holes in top with ice pick.
11. Pour liquid mixture over cake while still very warm.
12. Wrap tightly in foil or plastic wrap.

Directions for liquid mixture:

1. In small saucepan, heat mixture until sugar is dissolved.
2. Note: If heated long enough, all alcohol will evaporate and only the taste will remain for teetotalers.

German Chocolate Cake

This is a wonderful German chocolate cake.

Ingredients for cake:

1	pkg. German sweet chocolate
½	c. water, boiling
1	c. butter
2	c. sugar
4	eggs, separated
1	tsp. vanilla extract
2½	c. cake flour
1	tsp. baking powder
½	tsp. salt
1	c. buttermilk

Ingredients for frosting:

1	c. evaporated milk
1	c. sugar
3	egg yolks
¼	lb. butter
1	tsp. vanilla extract
1⅓	c. coconut
1	c. pecans, chopped

Directions for cake:

1. Preheat oven to 350 degrees F.
2. Line three 9-inch baking pans with wax paper.
3. Melt chocolate in boiling water; cool.
4. In large bowl, cream butter and sugar until light and fluffy.
5. Add egg yolks, one at a time, beating after each.
6. Add vanilla and melted chocolate; blend well.
7. In medium bowl, sift flour, baking soda, and salt together; add to chocolate mixture alternately with buttermilk, beating after each addition until smooth.
8. Fold in stiffly beaten egg whites.
9. Pour batter into prepared baking pans.
10. Bake 30 to 35 minutes.

Directions for frosting:

1. Combine all ingredients in saucepan.
2. Stir over medium heat 12 minutes until thickened.
3. Beat until cool enough to spread on top and between cooled layers of cake.

Orange Strawberry Shortcake

This makes a refreshing contrast of flavors with the ginger and orange creating a delicious and flavorful combination for this shortcake.

Ingredients:

2 c. flour
2 Tbs. sugar
1 Tbs. baking powder
½ tsp. baking soda
¼ tsp. salt
½ c. butter
2 Tbs. crystallized ginger, finely chopped
1 Tbs. fresh ginger, finely chopped
1 Tbs. orange zest
½ c. sour cream
¼ c. milk
  milk
  sugar

Directions:

1. Preheat oven to 425 degrees F.
2. In large bowl, sift flour, sugar, baking powder, baking soda, and salt together.
3. Using pastry blender or 2 knives, cut in butter until mixture resembles coarse crumbs.
4. Add crystallized ginger, fresh ginger, and zest.
5. In small bowl, whisk together sour cream and milk.
6. Add all at once to dry mixture, stirring with fork to make soft, slightly sticky dough.
7. Gather into ball and place on lightly floured surface.
8. Knead gently 8 times or until smooth; let rest 10 minutes.
9. Roll out into 8-inch circle and gently lift onto baking sheet.
10. Lightly brush dough with a small amount of milk and sprinkle with sugar.
11. Bake 20 minutes until top is golden brown.
12. Remove from oven and place on wire rack to cool.
13. Serve with your favorite toppings and sweetened whipped cream.

Jewish Apple Cake

This moist cake with cinnamon and sugar between the layers is always a favorite.

Ingredients for cake:

2   c. sugar
4   eggs
2½ tsp. vanilla extract
1   c. canola oil (not olive oil)
3   c. flour, sifted
3   tsp. baking powder
1¼ c. nuts, chopped
3   c. apples, finely chopped

Ingredients for cinnamon mix:

8   Tbs. sugar
3   tsp. cinnamon

Directions:

1. Preheat oven to 350 degrees F.
2. Grease and lightly flour a tube or bundt pan.
3. In large bowl, with electric mixer on high speed, beat sugar, eggs, vanilla, and oil for 10 minutes.
4. In another bowl, sift flour and baking powder together; add to sugar mixture.
5. Pour ⅓ of batter on bottom of prepared pan.
6. Combine nuts and apples; sprinkle half over batter.
7. Sprinkle with half of the sugar and cinnamon.
8. Add another ⅓ of batter, top with remaining nuts and apples, sprinkle with remainder of sugar and cinnamon, and add remaining ⅓ of the batter.
9. Bake 1¼ hours, or until inserted toothpick comes out clean.
10. If cake begins to brown too much, cover with foil.
11. Remove from oven, let stand 10 minutes in pan, and then turn out onto wire rack.
12. When cooled completely, dust with powdered sugar or frost with a drizzle icing.

Coconut Java Cake

My dad used to love this cake. My mom would make it for him on special occasions.

Ingredients for cake:

2¼ c. cake flour
1½ c. sugar
3 tsp. baking powder
1 tsp. salt
½ c. butter
1 c. strong coffee, cold
1½ tsp. vanilla extract
2 eggs

Ingredients for frosting:

½ c. brown sugar
¼ c. light corn syrup
2 Tbs. water
2 egg whites
1 tsp. vanilla extract
   grated coconut, sweetened

Directions for cake:

1. Preheat oven to 350 degrees F.
2. Lightly grease and flour two round 8 or 9-inch baking pans, or use wax paper and grease.
3. In large bowl, add brown sugar, corn syrup, water, egg whites, and vanilla.
4. With electric mixer on low speed, blend for 30 seconds, scraping bowl constantly.
5. Beat 3 minutes on high, scraping bowl occasionally.
6. Pour into prepared baking pans.
7. Bake 30 to 35 minutes.

Directions for frosting:

1. In small saucepan, combine sugar, water, and syrup.
2. Cover; over medium heat, bring to rolling boil.
3. Cook until dipping and removing a spoon in mixture spins a thread 6 to 8 inches long.
4. Pour hot syrup slowly over stiffly beaten egg whites, beating constantly on medium, until stiff peaks form.
5. Add vanilla.
6. Spread over cake layers, with lots of coconut on sides and top of cake.

Did You Know? . . . .

Did you know you can ensure a longer lasting Christmas tree by simply removing the bottom 2 inches of your tree trunk before placing the tree in the stand? This enables your tree to absorb water. Then by using a special tree preserving solution like the one below for every other watering, you can keep your tree soft and fresh. Just follow the directions to make your own solution.

Remember, however, to never, never let the water reservoir go dry.

Tree Preserving Solution

Ingredients:

1 Tbs. bleach
1 c. white corn syrup
1 gal. hot water

Directions:

1. *Boil water; stir in corn syrup and bleach.*
2. *Let cool slightly and add to tree reservoir every other watering.*

Dark Fruitcake

You will enjoy this delicious fruitcake, rich with holiday tradition.

Ingredients:

  2 c. flour
  1 tsp. baking powder
  ½ tsp. baking soda
  ¼ tsp. salt
  1 tsp. ground cinnamon
  1 tsp. ground nutmeg
  ½ tsp. ground mace
  ½ tsp. ground cloves
  ½ lb. butter
  2 c. brown sugar, packed
  6 lg. eggs
  ½ c. molasses
  ½ c. brandy
  2½ c. mixed candied fruits, diced (citron, pineapple,
     cherries, kumquats, and/or orange and lemon peel)
  2 c. walnuts, coarsely chopped
  1½ c. dates, chopped
  1½ c. currants
  1½ c. golden raisins
     grated zest and juice of 1 lemon
     grated zest and juice of 1 orange

Directions:

1. Have all ingredients at room temperature.
2. Preheat oven to 300 degrees F.
3. Grease and line bottom and sides of 10-inch tube
   pan with wax or parchment paper.
4. In large bowl, sift flour, baking powder, baking
   soda, salt, cinnamon, nutmeg, mace, and cloves
   together.

5. In another large bowl, with electric mixer on low speed, cream butter 30 seconds.
6. Gradually add brown sugar and beat on high until lightened in color and texture, 3 to 5 minutes.
7. Beat in eggs, one at a time, scraping sides of bowl.
8. Beat in molasses, grated zest, and citrus juices.
9. Add flour mixture in 2 parts alternately with brandy in 2 parts, beating on low speed or stirring with rubber spatula just until blended.
10. Scrape sides of bowl and stir in candied fruits, walnuts, dates, currants, and raisins.
11. Scrape batter into prepared pan and spread evenly.
12. Bake 3½ hours. Cake may appear done at 2½ hours; simply ignore this.
13. If cake is getting too dark on top, tent loosely with aluminum foil for last 30 to 60 minutes.
14. Cool in pan on rack for 1 hour.
15. Invert cake and remove paper liner; cool right side up on rack.
16. Note: This fruitcake is best stored for at least 1 month, but can be eaten sooner.
17. To store, wrap in plastic wrap or clean brandy or wine-soaked linens.
18. Cloth-wrapped cakes should be wrapped in plastic or heavy-duty sealable plastic bags.
19. Do not use aluminum foil to wrap liquor-dosed fruitcakes. The alcohol-fruit combination tends to dissolve foil.

Did You Know? . . . .

Did you know that the greater part of our happiness or our misery depends on our dispositions and not on our circumstances?

Did You Know? . . . .

Did you know who made that famous quote? ~ Martha Washington ~Born June 21, 1732. A very wise lady.

Poppy Seed Butter Cake

Poppy seed recipes come from my Yugoslavian and Czechoslovakian ancestry. This particular cake is very delicious. This version uses butter instead of shortening and also has a simple frosting. If you prefer, leave off the frosting and dust with powdered sugar.

Ingredients for cake:

1   c. butter, softened
1½ c. sugar
1   can ground poppy seed filling
4   eggs, separated
2   tsp. vanilla extract
1   c. sour cream
2½ c. flour
1   tsp. baking soda
1   tsp. salt

Ingredients for frosting:

4   Tbs. flour
1   c. milk
1   c. butter
1   c. sugar
1   tsp. vanilla extract

Directions for cake:

1. Preheat oven to 350 degrees F.
2. Grease and flour a 12-cup bundt pan or a 10-inch tube pan; set aside.
3. In large bowl, with electric mixer, beat butter and sugar light and fluffy.
4. Add poppy seed filling and beat until blended.
5. Beat in egg yolks, one at a time, beating well after each addition.

6. Add vanilla and sour cream; beat just until blended.
7. Stir flour, baking soda, and salt until mixed.
8. Add to poppy seed mixture gradually, beating well after each addition.
9. In separate bowl, with electric mixer, beat egg whites until stiff peaks form; fold into batter.
10. Spread batter evenly in prepared pan.
11. Bake 60 to 75 minutes, or until inserted toothpick in center comes out clean.
12. Remove from oven and cool in pan on wire rack 10 minutes.
13. Invert pan onto wire rack and cool completely.

Directions for frosting:

1. In small saucepan, boil flour and milk together until thick; cool to room temperature.
2. In small bowl, cream butter, sugar, salt, and vanilla.
3. Mix with flour and milk mixture.
4. Spread over cake, or if you prefer, dust cake with powdered sugar.

Did You Know? . . . .

Did you know that in 1949, the tree at Rockefeller Center was strung with 7,500 bulbs? Now more than 25,000 bulbs are strung on the tree - that's more than 5 miles of lights.

Did You Know? . . . .

Did you know that artificial Christmas trees were on the market by 1900? They were available by mail from Sears, Roebuck and Company, and cost 50 cents for 33 limbs, or a dollar for 55 limbs.

Streusel Filled Coffee Cake

This is an easy-to-make coffee cake with a great streusel filling.

Ingredients for cake:

1½ c. flour
¾ c. sugar
2½ tsp. baking powder
¾ tsp. salt
¼ c. butter
¾ c. milk
1 egg

Ingredients for filling:

½ c. brown sugar
2 tsp. cinnamon
¾ c. nuts, chopped
3 Tbs. butter, melted

Directions:

1. Preheat oven to 375 degrees F.
2. Lightly grease a 9-inch round layer or 8 or 9-inch square baking pan.
3. In large bowl, combine all cake ingredients and beat vigorously for 30 seconds.
4. Spread half the batter in prepared pan.
5. In small bowl, combine filling ingredients together and sprinkle half over batter in the pan.
6. Top with remaining batter, then remaining brown sugar mixture.
7. Bake 25 to 30 minutes, or until inserted toothpick in center comes out clean.

Yields: 16 servings.

Candies

Table of Contents

Page

Apple Gumdrops

These delicious old-fashioned gumdrops can be made right in your own home where the children can have fun helping.

Ingredients:

> 1 c. sugar
> 1 c. light corn syrup
> ¾ c. apple cider
> 1 pkg. powdered fruit pectin
> ½ tsp. baking soda
> 2 drops red food coloring (optional)
>   sugar
>   canola oil

Directions:

1. Line a 9 x 5 x 3-inch loaf pan with aluminum foil.
2. Brush the foil with oil.
3. In medium saucepan, over medium heat, heat sugar and corn syrup to boiling, stirring constantly until sugar is dissolved.
4. Bring to boil and cook, without stirring, to 280 degrees F. on candy thermometer, or until small amount of mixture dropped in cold water forms a hard ball.
5. In a small saucepan, heat apple cider, pectin, and baking soda to boiling.
6. Remove from heat and add to sugar mixture.
7. Stir in food coloring and let stand 2 minutes.
8. Skim off foam.
9. Pour mixture into prepared loaf pan, and let stand uncovered at room temperature for 24 hours.
10. Remove foil from pan.
11. With sharp knife dipped in sugar, cut into ¾-inch squares.

12. Roll squares in sugar.
13. Let stand at room temperature 1 hour.
14. Store gumdrops in airtight container.
15. Note: You can cut gumdrops into different shapes, just as you would cookies.

Almond Roca

This is an old family recipe I have made during the Christmas season for years. Wherever I take it during the holidays, it's usually the first thing gone. I hope you enjoy this treat as much as we do.

Ingredients:

2 c. brown sugar (1 lb.)
1 tsp. salt
½ c. water
1 c. butter
1 lg. chocolate candy bar, melted
1 c. almonds, chopped (optional)

Directions:

1. In small saucepan, combine brown sugar, salt, water, and butter.
2. Cook on medium heat about 8 minutes to hard crack stage, 300 degrees F., stirring constantly.
3. Boil about 8 minutes.
4. Reduce heat 2 notches until done, about 10 minutes more.
5. Remove from heat.
6. Stir in chopped almonds if desired.
7. Pour very quickly onto large buttered baking sheet.
8. Cool.
9. Cover both sides with melted chocolate bar.

Blobs

These were one of my favorite sweet treats when I was a child. My aunt used to make them for me and they were a hit when I brought them to group meetings for kids.

Ingredients:

- 1 c. white corn syrup
- 1 c. sugar
- 7 c. Special K cereal
- 1 c. creamy peanut butter
- 1 c. butter
- 1 c. butterscotch chips
- 1 c. chocolate chips

Directions:

1. Butter a large saucepan and add syrup and sugar; bring to boil.
2. Add cereal and peanut butter; mix well.
3. In small saucepan, melt butter, butterscotch, and chocolate chips.
4. Pour over cereal mixture.
5. Drop by spoonfuls on wax paper, or put into a buttered 9 x 13-inch baking pan.

Caramels

Homemade caramels are delicious. Try this easy recipe and you will never want to eat store-bought caramels again.

Ingredients:

- 1 c. sugar
- ¾ c. dark corn syrup
- ½ c. butter

1   c. light cream, divided
1½ c. pecans or walnuts, chopped
1½ tsp. vanilla extract

Directions:

1. In large saucepan, combine sugar, syrup, butter, and ½ cup cream.
2. Bring to boil, stirring constantly.
3. Continue stirring while adding remaining ½ cup cream, and cook slowly to very hard-ball stage.
4. Add nuts and vanilla and pour into a buttered pan.
5. When firm, cut into squares of size desired.
6. Wrap each square with pieces of plastic wrap or wax paper for storing.

Mound Bars

My children love these mound bars from time to time. My high school friend used to make these.

Ingredients:

½ c. butter, melted
2 c. graham crackers, crushed
4 Tbs. sugar
2 c. coconut
1 can milk, condensed
1 pkg. chocolate chips (6 oz.)

Directions:

1. Preheat oven to 350 degrees F.
2. In small baking pan, combine butter, graham crackers, and sugar.
3. Bake 7 minutes (do not turn off oven).
4. Mix coconut and condensed milk; pour over graham cracker mixture.
5. Bake an additional 15 minutes.
6. Melt chocolate chips and pour on top of bars.

Best Chocolate Fudge

This fudge recipe is the best one I've tried. It is creamy, has great-tasting chocolate, and is packed with walnuts. Try using milk chocolate or dark chocolate to suit your taste. This is another family favorite.

Ingredients:

2¼ c. chocolate chips
3   c. fresh walnuts, chopped in large pieces
1   lg. can evaporated milk
1   jar marshmallow crème (9 oz.)
3   tsp. vanilla extract
1   c. butter
4½ c. sugar

Directions:

1. Butter a 9 x 13 x 2-inch baking pan.
2. Cover with wax paper, and butter the wax paper.
3. In large bowl, combine all ingredients except milk and sugar. Be sure the butter, marshmallow crème, and chocolate bits are at room temperature or slightly warmer.
4. In large saucepan, combine milk and sugar.
5. Bring to rolling boil on as low a heat as possible.
6. Boil (low) for 11 minutes, stirring constantly with wooden spoon.
7. It may turn brown, so don't be alarmed.
8. Pour mixture over ingredients in large bowl.
9. Mix quickly. Do not beat.
10. Pour into prepared baking pan.
11. Important: Remove mixture out of bowl and into pan as rapidly as possible.
12. Do not make substitutions.

Butterscotch Candy

Butterscotch is a favorite among many, and these candies are no exception. They are a bit like the old-fashioned peanut brittle, without the peanuts.

Ingredients:

1 c. brown sugar
¼ c. light corn syrup
1 c. water
¼ tsp. salt
⅓ c. butter
¼ tsp. vanilla extract

Directions:

1. In medium saucepan, combine sugar, corn syrup, water, and salt.
2. Stir over low heat until sugar dissolves.
3. Increase heat, and cook until thermometer registers 250 degrees F. or to firm-ball stage.
4. Add butter and continue cooking, occasionally stirring, until thermometer registers 300 degrees F.
5. Remove from heat, add vanilla, and pour into a lightly buttered shallow pan, making a layer ¼-inch deep.
6. While warm, score into squares with blunt butter knife.
7. When cool, break along scores into pieces.
8. May be stored in a cool place in an airtight jar.

Did You Know? . . . .

Did you know that a national biscuit company introduced "Barnum's Animal Crackers" as a holiday promotion in 1902? The string-carrying boxes were designed for hanging on the Christmas tree.

Chocolate Chip Peanut Butter Fudge

This is always easy to make and a favorite of many.

Ingredients:

4   c. sugar
1   jar marshmallow crème (7 oz.)
1½ c. evaporated milk
1   c. peanut butter, creamy or crunchy
1   Tbs. butter
1   c. semi-sweet or milk chocolate chips

Directions:

1. Line a 9 x 13-inch baking pan with aluminum foil, extending foil over edges of pan.
2. Butter foil lightly; set aside.
3. In heavy 4-quart saucepan, stir together sugar, marshmallow crème, evaporated milk, peanut butter, and butter.
4. Over medium heat, cook stirring constantly until mixture comes to full rolling boil.
5. Boil and stir 5 minutes, then remove from heat.
6. Immediately add chocolate chips, stir until smooth.
7. Pour into prepared pan; cool until firm.
8. Use foil to lift fudge out of pan; peel off foil.
9. Cut fudge into squares.
10. Store in tightly covered container in cool, dry place.
11. Note: For best results, do not double this recipe.

Yields: 8 dozen pieces.

Did You Know?

Did you know that North American real Christmas trees are grown in all 50 states and in Canada?

Chocolate Raspberry Truffles

The most beloved of French candies, truffles are fast becoming one of our favorites too. Our version has an optional cocoa powder dusting or a crunchy hazelnut outer coating.

Ingredients:

¾ c. butter, unsalted
1 lb. semi-sweet chocolate, finely chopped
½ c. seedless raspberry jam
¼ c. black raspberry liqueur or raspberry Chambord
½ c. Dutch process cocoa powder (optional)
1 c. hazelnuts, roasted, finely chopped

Directions:

1. Cut butter into pieces; melt in top of double boiler or metal bowl over (but not touching) hot water.
2. Add chocolate, stirring occasionally until smooth.
3. Remove from heat.
4. Blend in raspberry jam and liqueur until smooth.
5. Cover; freeze until firm, about 2 hours; or refrigerate until firm, 4 hours or overnight.
6. Place cocoa or hazelnuts in a wide shallow pie pan.
7. Using a melon baller or a tablespoon, scoop a tablespoon of cold chocolate mixture between your palms and roll to form a round ball.
8. Roll in desired coating; place on sided baking sheet.
9. Repeat until all the chocolate mixture is gone.
10. Cover tightly with plastic wrap until ready to serve.
11. Remove from refrigerator 10 minutes before serving.
12. Note: This recipe may be prepared up to 5 days ahead if truffles are covered tightly and refrigerated.
13. May be frozen for up to 1 month, double wrapped in plastic.

Cranberry Balls

These cranberry balls are an enjoyable candy as well as a great treat for your sweeties.

Ingredients:

   12 oz. vanilla wafer cookies, crushed
   1 c. powdered sugar
   ¼ c. butter, softened
   ½ c. frozen cranberry juice concentrate, thawed
   ½ tsp. vanilla extract
   ½ c. pecans, chopped
   ½ c. dried cranberries or dried cherries, chopped
      additional powdered sugar and/or coconut

Directions:

   1. In medium bowl, combine crushed cookies and sugar; blend in butter.
   2. Stir in cranberry juice concentrate; add vanilla and chopped nuts.
   3. With hands, shape the mixture into bite-size balls.
   4. Roll or shake each ball in plastic bag with additional powdered sugar or coconut.
   5. Arrange cranberry balls in single layer on tray.
   6. Store uncovered overnight in refrigerator for best flavor.

Yields: 36 to 40 balls.

Did You Know? . . . .

Did you know the first Christmas card, created by a London businessman, was printed in England in 1843? Three years later, the first commercial Christmas cards were available to the public. One thousand cards in all were produced, and they were an instant success.

Divinity

My mom used to make this divinity recipe on holidays and special occasions.

Ingredients:

2½ c. sugar
½ c. light corn syrup
½ c. water
2   egg whites, stiffly beaten
1   tsp. vanilla extract
½ c. candied fruit
⅔ c. nuts, chopped
1-2 drops of red or green food coloring (optional)

Directions:

1. In heavy saucepan mix sugar, corn syrup, and water.
2. Cook and stir over medium-high heat to boiling.
3. Reduce heat to medium and cook without stirring 10 to 15 minutes, until candy reaches hard-ball stage; remove from heat.
4. Gradually pour hot mixture in a thin stream over stiffly beaten egg whites while beating on high about 3 minutes, scraping bowl as you beat mixture.
5. Add vanilla and, if desired, food coloring.
6. Continue beating on high just until candy starts to lose its gloss. When beaters are lifted, mixture should fall in a ribbon that mounds on itself.
7. This final beating should take 5 to 6 minutes.
8. Immediately stir in fruits or nuts.
9. Quickly drop remaining mixture by teaspoonfuls onto wax paper.
10. If mixture flattens out, beat for another ½ to 1 minute, then continue to spoon out.
11. If mixture is too stiff to spoon, beat in a few drops hot water until candy is a softer consistency.

Microwave Peanut Brittle

Adult supervision is needed for younger children who are working with this recipe. Peanut brittle is a holiday favorite. Try this easy microwave method.

Ingredients:

- 1   c. sugar
- ½ c. white corn syrup
- 1¼ c. dry roasted peanuts
- 1   tsp. butter
- 1   tsp. vanilla extract
- 1   tsp. baking soda

Directions:

1. Mix sugar and corn syrup in a 1½-quart casserole dish. Microwave on high for 4 minutes.
2. Stir in peanuts, microwave on high for 3 to 5 minutes, or until light brown.
3. Add butter and vanilla to syrup and peanut mixture.
4. Mix well, microwave on high for 1 to 2 minutes.
5. Use a pot holder, the bowl will be hot.
6. Add baking soda and stir until foamy.
7. Quickly pour mixture onto a lightly greased baking sheet. Let cool for 30 minutes to 1 hour.
8. Do not cool in refrigerator, as it might turn sugary and it won't be crunchy.

Pecan Butter Coconut Candy

This is a simple treat that children especially love, and it is so simple.

Ingredients:

- 1   pkg. butterscotch chips (12 oz.), melted

6 Tbs. peanut butter
4 c. corn flakes
2½ c. coconut

Directions:

1. In large bowl, combine butterscotch chips and peanut butter.
2. Add corn flakes and coconut; mix well.
3. Place into 9 x 13-inch buttered pan and cut in squares.

Turtles

This recipe is from my sister, Sandy. She liked making these for friends and family. They were always enjoyed by everyone.

Ingredients:

70 caramels
5 Tbs. cream
4½ c. pecans
2 giant chocolate bars
½ bar paraffin wax

Directions:

1. Melt caramels and cream in double boiler.
2. Stir in pecans.
3. Drop by teaspoons on greased baking sheet and freeze.
4. Melt chocolate bars and then add paraffin wax.
5. Dip frozen candy into chocolate and put on baking sheet.

Yields: 40 pieces.

Holiday Berry Mocha Fudge

The blend of raspberry and chocolate and coffee is so wonderful.

Ingredients:

¼   lb. butter
1   can evaporated milk (12 oz.)
3½ c. sugar
1½ Tbs. instant coffee
10 oz. raspberry chocolate chips
2   oz. bittersweet chocolate
7   oz. marshmallow crème
1   tsp. vanilla extract

Directions:

1. Melt butter in heavy saucepan.
2. Add evaporated milk, sugar, and coffee.
3. Bring to rolling boil, stirring constantly until the temperature reaches 235 degrees F. on a candy thermometer.
4. Remove from heat.
5. Add raspberry chips and bittersweet chocolate.
6. Stir mixture until all ingredients have melted.
7. Add marshmallow crème and stir until blended.
8. Stir in vanilla.
9. Pour into a lightly greased 9 x 13-inch baking pan.
10. Cut into bite-size pieces after fudge has cooled.

Did You Know? . . . .

Did you know that it's the idea of giving that reminds us we are all on this planet together, for the long run? So let's be kind to one another.

Molasses Taffy

This is a fun project for children. The family can enjoy pulling the taffy as they tell stories around the kitchen table.

Ingredients:

2 c. sugar
1 c. light molasses
¼ c. water
2 tsp. vinegar
2 Tbs. butter
½ tsp. baking soda

Directions:

1. Butter sides of heavy 2-quart saucepan.
2. In saucepan, combine sugar, molasses, and water.
3. Heat slowly, stirring constantly until sugar is dissolved.
4. Bring to boiling, add vinegar, and cook to light-crack stage.
5. Remove from heat, add butter, and sift in baking soda; stir.
6. Turn out (don't scrape) on buttered platter or large shallow pan.
7. For even cooling, use a spatula to turn the edges to the center.
8. Pull taffy while it's as warm as you can handle.
9. Use only finger tips to pull - if candy sticks, dip fingers in cornstarch.

Did You Know? . . . .

Did you know that an acre of Christmas trees produces the daily oxygen for 18 people?

Cranberry Fudge

Cranberries add great flavor and color to rich chocolate fudge.

Ingredients:

2 c. semi-sweet chocolate chips
¼ c. light corn syrup
½ c. powdered sugar
¼ c. evaporated milk
1 tsp. vanilla extract
1 pkg. sweetened dried cranberries (6 oz.)
1 c. pecans, chopped

Directions:

1. Line the bottom and sides of 8 x 8-inch baking pan with plastic wrap; set aside.
2. In medium saucepan, combine chocolate chips and corn syrup.
3. Cook over low heat until melted and smooth.
4. Remove from heat.
5. Add powdered sugar, evaporated milk, and vanilla.
6. Stir vigorously until the mixture is thick and glossy.
7. Add cranberries and nuts; mix well.
8. Pour into prepared pan.
9. Cover.
10. Chill 8 hours, or until firm.
11. Cut into 1½-inch squares.
12. Store covered in refrigerator.
13. Serve at room temperature.

Yields: 25 squares.

Christmas Delights Cookbook
A Collection of Christmas Recipes
Cookbook Delights Holiday Series Book 12

Cookies

Table of Contents

Page

Biscochitos

Try these uniquely-flavored cookies. The alcohol cooks out, so it is added for the flavor, not the alcohol.

Ingredients:

1½ c. sugar
1   lb. pure lard or shortening
3   eggs
1   oz. wine, brandy, or whiskey
7   c. flour
3   tsp. baking powder
½   tsp. salt
1   Tbs. anise seed, crushed
½   c. sugar
1   Tbs. cinnamon

Directions:

1. In large bowl, cream lard.
2. Add sugar, and cream again.
3. Add eggs, one at a time, beating into the creamed mixture.
4. Mix in the wine (or brandy, or whiskey).
5. Add flour, baking powder, salt, and anise; mix well.
6. Refrigerate overnight.
7. Preheat oven to 350 degrees F.
8. On a floured surface, roll out ¼-inch thick.
9. Cut into fancy shapes.
10. In small bowl, blend sugar and cinnamon together.
11. Dip the tops of the cookies in mixture.
12. Place on ungreased baking sheet.
13. Bake 12 minutes, or until light brown.
14. Cool.
15. Remove from baking sheet onto wire rack.

Yields: 5 dozen.

Butternut Ball Cookies

Use powdered sugar rather than granulated sugar to make these cookies more tender.

Ingredients:

- 1 c. butter, softened
- ¾ c. powdered sugar, sifted
- 2 tsp. vanilla extract
- 2⅓ c. flour
- ¼ tsp. salt
- pecan halves
- chocolate kisses

Directions:

1. Preheat oven to 400 degrees F.
2. In large bowl, combine butter and powdered sugar.
3. Mix well.
4. Add vanilla and beat.
5. Add dry ingredients and mix until a dough forms.
6. Form dough around pecan halves or chocolate kisses, enclosing nut or chocolate completely.
7. Bake on ungreased baking sheets 10 to 12 minutes.
8. Cookies should not brown.
9. Immediately drop into a bowl full of powdered sugar and roll to coat.
10. Let cool on wire racks.
11. When cool, roll in powdered sugar again.

Did You Know? . . . .

Did you know that for every real Christmas tree harvested, up to 3 seedlings are planted in its place the following spring?

Christmas Cookies

These are fun to make with your children. Make plenty to decorate with the kids.

Ingredients:

  1 c. butter
  1 c. sugar
  2 eggs
  2 tsp. vanilla extract
  ½ tsp. almond extract
  2½ c. flour, sifted
  2 tsp. baking powder
  ½ tsp. salt

Directions:

  1. In large bowl, combine all ingredients; chill.
  2. Preheat oven to 350 degrees F.
  3. Roll dough out onto a floured surface or cloth.
  4. Use cookie cutters to cut into shapes.
  5. Bake 10 minutes, or until lightly brown on edges.
  6. Sprinkle on colored sugar before baking, or you may frost after baking.

Christmas Cookies Casserole

Try this unique and easy-to-make cookie recipe for a fun cookie making project with children. They will especially enjoy leaving Santa some cookies that they helped make.

Ingredients:

  1 c. sugar
  3 eggs
  ½ tsp. salt

1¼ c. dates, cut up
1¼ c. coconut
1¼ c. walnuts, finely chopped
1   tsp. vanilla extract
     powdered sugar

Directions:

1. Preheat oven to 350 degrees F.
2. Grease casserole dish.
3. Mix first 7 ingredients together.
4. Bake for 25 minutes stirring several times.
5. Cool and stir again.
6. Form into small balls, and roll into powdered sugar.

Christmas Molasses Cookies

I love molasses cookies, and these are great with milk.

Ingredients:

⅔   c. butter
¾   c. sugar
1   egg
1   tsp. baking soda in 4 Tbs. milk
½   c. dark molasses
1   heaping tsp. cloves
1   heaping tsp. ginger
2   heaping tsp. cinnamon
¾   tsp. salt
1¾ c. flour, more if needed

Directions:

1. Preheat oven to 325 degrees F.
2. In large bowl, combine all ingredients together.
3. Drop unto greased baking sheet.
4. Bake 8 to 10 minutes.
5. Do not overcook; will not look done until cooled.

Christmas Oatmeal Cookies

Oatmeal cookies are always a welcome treat.

Ingredients:

¾　c. butter
1　c. brown sugar
½　c. sugar
1　egg
⅓　c. water
1　tsp. vanilla extract
1　c. flour
1　tsp. salt
½　tsp. baking soda
3½　c. oatmeal
1½ c. nuts, chopped
　　coconut (optional)

Directions:

1. Preheat oven to 350 degrees F.
2. In large bowl, combine all ingredients.
3. Add nuts or coconut if desired.
4. Drop by spoonfuls onto baking sheet.
5. Bake 10 to 15 minutes, or until edges are golden brown.

Christmas Peanut Butter Cookies

Peanut butter cookies are always popular with children.

Ingredients:

¼ c. butter
¾ c. peanut butter
½ c. sugar
½ c. brown sugar
1　egg
1　c. flour

½ tsp. baking soda
½ tsp. baking powder
¼ tsp. salt

Directions:

1. Preheat oven to 325 degrees F.
2. In large bowl, cream first 4 ingredients together.
3. Add egg and beat in well.
4. Sift dry ingredients and add to creamed mixture.
5. Drop by teaspoons onto greased baking sheet and press lightly with a sugar-dipped fork. Or roll into balls the size of walnuts and press down with fork.
6. Bake 15 to 20 minutes, or until done.

Yields: 3½ dozen.

Date Balls

My dad always loved dates, and my mom would make these date treats. These make a tasty date cookie.

Ingredients:

1   lb. dates, cut fine
1   c. sugar
2   eggs
3   c. rice cereal
1½ c. nuts, finely chopped

Directions:

1. Place dates, sugar, and eggs in a skillet.
2. Cook at 260 degrees F. for 10 minutes stirring constantly.
3. Turn off heat; add rice cereal and chopped nuts.
4. Mix well.
5. Butter hands and roll dough into balls.
6. Roll the balls in ground nuts, chopped coconut, or powdered sugar.

Gingerbread Boys and Girls

Christmas would not be complete without traditional gingerbread boys and girls.

Ingredients:

1	c. butter
1	c. sugar
½	tsp. salt
1	egg
1	c. molasses
2	Tbs. vinegar
5	c. flour, sifted
1½	tsp. baking soda
1	Tbs. ginger
1	tsp. cinnamon
1	tsp. cloves
2	c. powdered sugar
	half and half cream, to mix with powdered sugar

Directions:

1. In large bowl, cream butter, sugar, and salt.
2. Stir in egg, molasses, and vinegar; beat well.
3. In large bowl, sift dry ingredients; stir into creamed mixture; chill 3 hours.
4. Preheat oven to 375 degrees F.
5. Lightly grease baking sheets.
6. On lightly floured surface, roll dough out ⅛-inch thick.
7. Cut out with gingerbread boys and girls cutters.
8. Place 1 inch apart on prepared baking sheet.
9. Bake 6 minutes.
10. Cool slightly and remove from baking sheet.
11. When completely cool, decorate.
12. Add sufficient cream to 2 cups powdered sugar to make proper icing consistency.

Holiday Butter Cookies

This butter cookie recipe is a great choice to make cutout cookies.

Ingredients:

1   c. butter
1   c. sugar
1½ tsp. vanilla extract
1   egg
1   tsp. water
3   c. flour
1½ tsp. baking powder
¼   tsp. salt

Directions:

1. In large bowl, cream butter, sugar, and vanilla.
2. Add egg and water; beat until light and fluffy.
3. In medium bowl, sift flour, baking powder, and salt.
4. Add to creamed mixture.
5. Divide dough in half.
6. Chill 1 hour.
7. Preheat oven to 375 degrees F.
8. On lightly floured surface, roll dough to ⅛-inch thick.
9. Cut in desired shapes with 2½-inch cookie cutters and place on baking sheets.
10. Brush lightly with milk.
11. Sprinkle with colored sugar, candy decorettes or chopped nuts.
12. Bake 6 to 8 minutes.
13. Cool slightly; remove from pan.
14. Note: You can also bake the cookies plain and glaze with powdered sugar blended with milk.

Yields: 6 dozen.

Quick Cookies

This is another favorite cookie for children, and they are very quick and easy to make.

Ingredients:

3½ c. quick oats
½ c. cocoa
¾ c. walnuts
½ c. coconut
3 tsp. vanilla extract
1 tsp. salt
2 c. sugar
½ c. butter
¾ c. milk

Directions:

1. In medium bowl, combine oats, cocoa, walnuts, coconut, vanilla, and salt; set aside.
2. In medium saucepan, combine sugar, butter, and milk.
3. Bring to boil; boil 3½ minutes.
4. Add to oatmeal mixture and drop by spoonfuls on wax paper.

Yields: 42 cookies.

Raspberry Oatmeal Bars

Oatmeal and raspberries make a great taste combination, and the coconut adds texture and flavor.

Ingredients:

1¼ c. flour
1½ c. quick oats
½ c. sugar
½ tsp. baking soda
⅓ c. butter, melted
2 tsp. pure vanilla extract

1   c. coconut, shredded
    raspberry jam

Directions:

1. Preheat oven to 350 degrees F.
2. In large bowl, combine flour, oats, sugar, baking
   soda, butter, and vanilla to make crumb mixture.
3. Reserve 1 cup of mixture and press the rest on
   bottom of greased 9 x 13-inch baking pan.
4. Spread raspberry jam over top, then sprinkle
   coconut and the reserved crumb mixture over that.
5. Bake 25 minutes.
6. Cool completely before cutting into bars.

Press Cookies

*These spritz cookies are made with a press and are a
tradition in Europe on holidays, especially at tea time.*

Ingredients:

½ c. butter
1   pkg. cream cheese (3 oz.), softened
⅓ c. sugar
1   egg yolk
1   tsp. lemon extract
1½ c. flour
½ tsp. salt

Directions:

1. Preheat oven to 400 degrees F.
2. In large bowl, cream butter, cream cheese, and
   sugar until light and fluffy.
3. Add egg yolks and extract, beating well.
4. In small bowl, combine flour and salt together.
5. Add to creamed mixture in 3 additions, mixing well
   after each addition.
6. Fill cookie press and make desired shapes on
   ungreased baking sheets.
7. Bake 10 to 12 minutes, or until lightly browned.

Spritz Cookies

My mom used to make these delicious, buttery spritz cookies. Here are some variations for you to try also.

Ingredients:

⅔ c. sugar
1 c. butter, softened
1 egg
½ tsp. salt
2 tsp. vanilla extract
2¼ c. flour

Directions:

1. Preheat oven to 400 degrees F.
2. In large bowl, combine all ingredients except flour.
3. With electric mixer on medium speed, beat until creamy.
4. Reduce speed to low, add flour; and beat well.
5. If desired, prepare dough as directed by variations below.
6. If dough is too soft, cover and refrigerate 30 to 45 minutes.
7. Place dough into cookie press fitted with template.
8. Form desired shapes, place 1 inch apart, onto ungreased baking sheets.
9. Bake 6 to 8 minutes, or until edges are lightly browned.

Ingredient addition for chocolate chip spritz:

¼ c. semi-sweet chocolate, coarsely grated

Directions for chocolate chip spritz:

1. Mix in grated semi-sweet chocolate with the cookie dough.

Ingredient addition for eggnog glazed spritz:

1 tsp. ground nutmeg

1   c. powdered sugar
¼   c. butter, softened
2   Tbs. water
¼   tsp. rum extract

Directions for eggnog glazed spritz:

1. Mix nutmeg in with the cookie dough.
2. In small bowl, stir powdered sugar, butter, water, and rum extract together until smooth.
3. Drizzle over warm cookies.

Ingredient addition for Lebkuchen spice spritz:

1   tsp. ground cinnamon
1   tsp. ground nutmeg
½   tsp. ground allspice
¼   tsp. ground cloves
1   c. powdered sugar
2   Tbs. milk
½   tsp. vanilla extract

Directions for Lebkuchen spice spritz:

1. Add cinnamon, nutmeg, allspice, and cloves to the cookie dough.
2. In a small bowl, stir powdered sugar, milk, and vanilla together until smooth.
3. Drizzle over warm cookies.

Ingredient addition for mint kisses:

¼   tsp. peppermint extract
    chocolate candy kisses

Directions for mint kisses:

1. Add peppermint extract to the cookie dough.
2. Immediately after removing cookies from oven, place 1 chocolate candy kiss on each cookie.

Yields: 5 dozen.

Holiday Red Raspberry Chocolate Bars

The combination of red raspberries and chocolate make a great holiday treat.

Ingredients:

2½ c. flour
1   c. sugar
1   c. pecans, finely chopped
1   c. butter, cold
1   egg, beaten
1   jar red raspberry jam (12 oz.)
1⅔ c. chocolate chips (10 oz.)

Directions:

1. Preheat oven to 350 degrees F.
2. Grease 9 x 13-inch baking pan.
3. In large bowl, stir flour, sugar, pecans, butter, and egg together.
4. Cut in butter with pastry blender or fork until mixture resembles coarse crumbs.
5. Set aside 1½ cups crumb mixture.
6. Press remaining crumb mixture on bottom of prepared pan; spread jam over top.
7. Sprinkle with chocolate chips.
8. Crumble remaining crumb mixture evenly over top.
9. Bake 40 to 45 minutes, or until lightly browned.
10. Cool completely in pan on wire rack.
11. Cut into bars.

Yields: 3 dozen bars.

Did You Know? . . . .

Did you know there are approximately 30 to 35 million real Christmas trees sold in the U.S. every year?

Triple Chocolate Oatmeal Cookies

Triple chocolate and double nuts make these oatmeal cookies especially delightful.

Ingredients:

1¾ c. rolled oats, divided
8 Tbs. butter, unsalted, room temperature
½ c. sugar
½ c. brown sugar, firmly packed
1 egg
1 tsp. vanilla extract
1 c. flour
½ tsp. baking powder
½ tsp. baking soda
¼ tsp. salt
3 oz. milk chocolate, chopped
3 oz. dark chocolate chips
3 oz. white chocolate, chopped
½ c. almonds, blanched, chopped
½ c. pecans, chopped

Directions:

1. Preheat oven to 375 degrees F.
2. Place 1½ cups oats in container of food processor and process 1 minute until fine.
3. In large bowl, with electric mixer, beat butter with both sugars until smooth.
4. Beat in egg and vanilla.
5. Combine processed oats with flour, baking powder, baking soda, and salt.
6. Slowly add to butter mixture.
7. Stir in remaining ¼ cup oats, chocolates, almonds, and pecans.
8. Drop by spoonfuls onto ungreased baking sheets.
9. Bake 10 minutes, or until golden brown.
10. Cool slightly on baking sheets before removing.

Yields: 40 cookies.

Viennese Crescent Cookies

This is a great holiday cookie for family and guests to enjoy.

Ingredients:

- 4 c. flour
- 2 c. butter
- 2 c. hazelnuts, ground
- 1 c. powdered sugar, sifted
- ¼ tsp. salt
- 2 tsp. vanilla extract
- 4 c. powder sugar, sifted
- 2 whole vanilla beans

Directions:

1. Preheat oven to 375 degrees F.
2. In large mixing bowl, combine flour, butter, nuts, ½ cup of sugar, salt, and extracts.
3. Hand mix until thoroughly blended.
4. Shape dough into ball, cover, and refrigerate 1 hour.
5. Meanwhile, place sugar in a bowl.
6. With sharp, pointed knife, split vanilla bean lengthwise; scrape out seeds, mix seeds into sugar.
7. Cut pod into 2-inch pieces and mix into sugar.
8. Remove dough from refrigerator and form into 1-inch balls. With palms of hands, roll each ball into a small roll 3 inches long.
9. Place rolls 2 inches apart on ungreased baking sheet. Curve each roll to make a crescent shape.
10. Bake 10 to 12 minutes, or until set, but not brown.
11. Let stand 1 minute, and then remove from baking sheets. With spatula, place hot cookie on large sheet of foil. Sprinkle with prepared sugar mixture.
12. Turn gently to coat on both sides. Cool.
13. Store in airtight container.
14. Just before serving, coat with more vanilla sugar mixture, if desired.

Christmas Delights Cookbook
A Collection of Christmas Recipes
Cookbook Delights Holiday Series Book 12

Desserts

Table of Contents

Page

Apple Strudel

I have fond memories of my mother making homemade apple strudel when I was young. This is one of the easier recipes and definitely worth making. It is great served warm out of the oven with vanilla ice cream and dusted with fresh-ground cinnamon.

Ingredients:

2	c. flour
1	tsp. salt
2	Tbs. shortening
1	Tbs. canola oil
¼	c. water, warm
2	eggs
12	apples, chopped or finely grated
⅓	lb. butter, melted
1	c. sugar
1½	tsp. cinnamon

Directions:

1. Sift flour into bowl and form a well.
2. Into the well put the salt, shortening, canola oil, warm water, and 2 eggs.
3. Work into the flour gradually.
4. After thorough mixing, cover with a warm, wet cloth and let stand 1 hour.
5. Preheat oven to 400 degrees F.
6. Roll dough very thin, until it covers a circle about 28 to 30 inches in diameter.
7. Brush half the melted butter onto the thin stretched dough.
8. Sprinkle on the apples.
9. Sprinkle on sugar and rest of butter.
10. Roll tight as you would a jellyroll.
11. Tuck in corners tightly.

12. Shape dough into a horseshoe shape.
13. Lightly grease a large baking pan with sides.
14. Place dough in prepared pan.
15. Bake 10 minutes; reduce heat to 350 degrees F.
16. Bake 50 minutes, or until done.
17. Sprinkle powdered sugar on top or frost after cooling.

Chocolate Dipped Strawberries

Two of my daughters enjoy making these strawberries, and the entire family enjoys them. These strawberries add a festive touch to the holiday season and make great gifts.

Ingredients:

2 c. semi-sweet chocolate chips
1 Tbs. shortening
1 Tbs. butter
    fresh strawberries with stems, rinsed, patted dry

Directions:

1. Cover a tray with wax paper.
2. In medium microwave-safe bowl, place chocolate chips.
3. Microwave on high for 1½ minutes, or just until chips are melted and mixture is smooth when stirred.
4. Cool slightly.
5. Holding strawberry by top, dip ⅔ of each berry into chocolate mixture.
6. Shake gently to remove excess.
7. Place on prepared tray.
8. Refrigerate 30 minutes, or until coating is firm.
9. Serve within 24 hours.

Chocolate Raspberry Cream Crêpes

These chocolate crêpes are excellent with the raspberry cream sauce.

Ingredients for crêpes:

3   eggs
¼   c. sugar
1   c. flour
1   c. milk
1   Tbs. cocoa powder
1   Tbs. butter, melted
1   Tbs. vanilla extract

Ingredients for white sauce:

6   oz. white chocolate baking bar
5   Tbs. whipping cream
2   Tbs. light corn syrup
1½ Tbs. raspberry liqueur
½   tsp. vanilla extract

Ingredients for raspberry cream:

1   c. whipping cream
1   Tbs. raspberry liqueur
1   Tbs. sugar
2   pt. fresh raspberries
    fresh mint sprigs, for garnish

Directions for crêpes:

1. In blender or food processor, add all ingredients for crêpes; process until smooth.
2. Heat 6-inch skillet over medium heat, coat with canola spray.

3. Pour 2 to 3 tablespoons batter in skillet, swirling to form crepe.
4. Cook 1 minute on each side, or until golden.
5. Repeat with remaining batter.
6. Crêpes may be stacked and freeze well.

Directions for white sauce:

1. In small saucepan, over low heat, gently melt chocolate, stirring at intervals. Set aside.
2. In another small saucepan, bring cream to boil.
3. Add corn syrup, stirring until blended.
4. Gradually add cream mixture to melted chocolate, stirring until smooth.
5. Stir in liqueur and vanilla.
6. Keep warm.

Directions for raspberry cream:

1. In large bowl, with electric mixer, whip cream, raspberry liqueur, and sugar to form peaks.
2. Fold in ¼ of raspberries.
3. Spoon some chocolate sauce over center of each dessert plate.
4. Spoon a generous 2 tablespoons raspberry cream down center of each crêpe.
5. Fold two sides over and place seam side down on chocolate sauce.
6. Sprinkle with raspberries and garnish with mint.
7. Serve immediately.

Yields: 14 crêpes.

Did you Know? . . . .

Did you know that you can locate the nearest recycling program by logging onto www.realchristmastrees.org or calling 1-800-CLEANUP?

Christmas Pudding

Christmas pudding is traditionally made on Stir-up Sunday, which is the last Sunday before Advent. The best puddings are then allowed to mature until Christmas.

Ingredients for pudding:

1   c. flour, self-rising
1   lb. bread crumbs
1   lb. suet
1   lb. dark brown sugar
1   tsp. allspice
1½ c. currants, washed (12 oz.)
3   c. raisins, washed (24 oz.)
1½ c. sultanas, washed (12 oz.)
¾   c. mixed peel (6 oz.)
¼   c. almonds, ground
¼   tsp. fresh nutmeg, grated
8   eggs
2   cans stout beer (Guinness)
1   measure of brandy
3   Tbs. black treacle or dark molasses
1   carrot, grated
1   cooking apple, grated
1   baking potato, grated
    grated rind of 2 lemons
    juice of 3 oranges

Ingredients for brandy butter:

¾   c. butter, unsalted
¾   c. dark brown sugar, soft
6   Tbs. brandy

Directions for pudding:

1. In large mixing bowl, place all dry ingredients and grated items. Make a well in the center of the bowl.
2. In small bowl, whisk together eggs and treacle. Place into the well.

3. Bind all ingredients together, traditionally by using your hands rather than a spoon.
4. Once well bound, add all liquid ingredients to the bowl and mix very well. The mixture should be of a "dropping" consistency.
5. Add more liquid of your choice to adjust to taste and required consistency.
6. Allow pudding to soak overnight.
7. The following day, add a teaspoon of baking powder and also some extra alcohol, as much of it will have been absorbed overnight.
8. To cook, place in a well-greased pudding basin.
9. Allow a 1-inch space from the top for the pudding to rise slightly.
10. On top of the pudding place a double layer of greased, greaseproof paper.
11. Seal the top with a layer of tinfoil secured with an elastic band.
12. Steam the Christmas pudding in a double steamer initially for 10 hours.
13. Let the pudding cool and store until required.

To finish cooking:

1. On Christmas Day, place the pudding in a double steamer for another 5 hours.
2. Turn the pudding out onto a large plate and flame with brandy.
3. Note: Warm the brandy slightly before pouring over the pudding.
4. Serve with traditional brandy butter.

Directions for brandy butter:

1. In medium bowl, beat butter and sugar together until creamy.
2. Gradually add the brandy to the mixture, ensuring that after each addition you beat the mixture well to prevent the butter from curdling.
3. Place mixture into a covered container.
4. Chill at least 1 hour before serving.
5. The brandy butter will keep for up to two weeks in the refrigerator, so it can be made well ahead of Christmas Day.

Classic Crème Brûleè

This is an easy-to-make, but very rich custard.

Ingredients:

    8 egg yolks
    ⅓ c. sugar
    2 c. heavy cream
    1 tsp. pure vanilla extract

Directions:

1. Preheat oven to 300 degrees F.
2. In large bowl, combine egg yolks and sugar; whisk together until the sugar has dissolved and mixture is thick and pale yellow.
3. Add cream and vanilla, and continue to whisk until well blended.
4. Strain into large bowl, skimming off any foam or bubbles.
5. Divide mixture among 6 ramekins or custard cups.
6. Place in water bath and bake 40 to 50 minutes, or until set around edges, but still loose in center.
7. Remove from oven; leave in water bath until cooled.
8. Remove cups from water bath and chill at least 2 hours, or up to 2 days.
9. To serve, sprinkle 2 teaspoons sugar over each custard.
10. For best results, use small hand torch to melt the sugar. If you don't have a torch, place ramekins under broiler until sugar melts.
11. Rechill custards a few minutes before serving.

Yields: 6 servings.

Cherry Apple Crisp

This recipe is great during the winter months when the days are long and cold, and fresh fruit is out of season. Try this served warm with sweetened whipped cream or a scoop of vanilla ice cream on top.

Ingredients for filling:

- 1   can cherries, dark sweet, pitted
- ¾   c. cornstarch
- ¾   c. sugar
- 1½ qt. canned apples, sliced, drained
- 2   tsp. vanilla extract
- 1   Tbs. ground cinnamon
- ½   tsp. salt

Ingredients for topping:

- 4   c. old-fashioned rolled oats
- 2   c. flour
- 2   c. brown sugar, packed
- 1   c. butter, softened

Directions for filling:

1. Drain cherries; reserve syrup.
2. In large saucepan, combine reserved syrup, cornstarch, and sugar; bring mixture to boil.
3. Stir in drained cherries, apples, vanilla, cinnamon, and salt.

Directions for topping:

1. Preheat oven to 375 degrees F.
2. In large bowl, combine oats, flour, and brown sugar.
3. Cut in butter and mix until crumbly.
4. Pour warm cherry mixture into 12 x 20 x 2-inch baking pan.
5. Sprinkle oat topping over fruit.
6. Bake 30 to 35 minutes, or until topping is golden brown and fruit is bubbling hot.

Crêpe Suzette

Homemade crêpe Suzette is an elegant dessert for that special holiday gathering.

Ingredients for crêpes:

1   c. flour
4   lg. eggs
1¼ c. milk
1   pinch of salt
¼   c. butter, unsalted
    canola oil, for oiling pans

Ingredients for sauce:

¼   c. butter, unsalted
3   Tbs. sugar
1   orange, juice, and grated rind
⅓   c. orange liqueur (Cointreau or Grand Marnier)

Directions for crêpes:

1. In blender, combine flour, eggs, milk, and salt; blend just until smooth.
2. Add melted butter and combine.
3. Batter should be the consistency of light cream.
4. Let sit in refrigerator at least 1 hour or overnight.
5. Lightly oil 6-inch crêpe pan; set over medium heat.
6. Pour ¼ cup batter into pan; swirl until pan is coated.
7. Cook crêpes 60 seconds, or until the top begins to look dry.
8. Turn and cook other side 30 seconds, wiping pan with an oiled paper towel if crêpes begin to stick.

Directions for sauce:

1. In large skillet, melt butter.

2. When foamy, add sugar and stir until dissolved.
3. Add rind and juice; bring to simmer.
4. Reduce heat to lowest setting.
5. Fold each crepe in half and place 2 at a time in the warm sauce.
6. Using tongs or spatula, fold crêpes in half again.
7. Repeat until all crêpes have been added.
8. Work quickly so the first crêpes do not absorb all the sauce.
9. Warm liqueur briefly and pour over pan of crêpes.
10. Using a long match, ignite the sauce.
11. Remove pan from heat. When flames subside, place crêpes on dessert plates.
12. Dust with powdered sugar.
13. Garnish with orange slices and serve.

Yields: 4 servings.

Fig Pudding

This is an easy fig pudding to make for the holidays.

Ingredients:

½ lb. figs, finely chopped
⅓ c. butter
¼ lb. bread, grated
⅓ c. powdered sugar
2 eggs
1 c. milk
   bread crumbs

Directions:

1. In small bowl, mix figs with butter; add bread, powdered sugar, eggs, and milk.
2. Put in a buttered mold, sprinkle with bread crumbs, cover tightly, and boil for 3 hours.

Dark Chocolate Pavé with Raspberry

This memorable combination of dark chocolate, orange, and raspberry is perfect for the fanciest of dinner parties. It is also easy to prepare and can be made ahead.

Ingredients for pavé:

 2 c. milk
 6 oz. bittersweet chocolate
 1 c. sugar
 ½ c. butter
 1 c. cocoa
 1 tsp. orange flavoring or 2 drops orange oil
 2 tsp. gelatin, unflavored
 3 Tbs. water, cold
 1 c. heavy whipping cream

Ingredients for raspberry sauce:

 3 pkg. raspberries (10 oz. ea.), frozen in syrup, thawed
 ½ c. sugar
 1½ Tbs. cornstarch
    juice of ½ orange

Directions for pavé:

1. Prepare 8½ x 4½-inch loaf pan by lining bottom and long sides with double layer of wax paper which extends over each edge of pan.
2. Set aside.
3. In small heavy saucepan over medium-low heat, bring milk to simmering.
4. Add bittersweet chocolate, and stir occasionally until chocolate is melted and mixture is smooth.
5. Add sugar, butter, and cocoa; whisk until completely dissolved. Do not allow mixture to boil.

6. When mixture looks smooth, strain into medium bowl, add orange flavoring, and set aside to cool.
7. In small heatproof cup, sprinkle gelatin over cold water and allow mixture to soften for 2 to 3 minutes.
8. Microwave gelatin mixture on high for 20 seconds and allow to stand for 2 minutes or until granules are completely dissolved.
9. Blend into chocolate mixture and set aside.
10. Beat heavy cream in chilled bowl with chilled beaters until nearly stiff and peaks hold their shape.
11. Cool chocolate mixture to room temperature and fold in whipped cream.
12. Pour into loaf pan and freeze 6 hours or overnight.

Directions for raspberry sauce:

1. In blender or food processor, process undrained berries and orange juice until smooth.
2. Strain through a sieve.
3. In small saucepan, blend sugar, cornstarch, and strained berries.
4. Over medium heat, bring to simmer stirring frequently.
5. Reduce heat and continue stirring until sauce thickens.
6. Remove from heat; cool.
7. To serve, remove from freezer 20 minutes before serving.
8. Place 2 to 3 tablespoons raspberry sauce on each dessert plate.
9. Slice with clean knife dipped in warm water and place slice on each plate.
10. Garnish with thin slices of orange zest and partially frozen, whole frozen raspberries.
11. Pass any extra raspberry sauce around the table.

Yields: 16 slices pavé, 3 cups sauce.

Huckleberry Crisp

This is very tasty and best served right out of the oven.

Ingredients:

5 c. huckleberries
¼ c. sugar
½ tsp. lemon rind, grated
1 c. apples, peeled, diced
½ c. light brown sugar
2 tsp. cinnamon
1 tsp. nutmeg
½ c. flour
½ c. rolled oats
⅛ tsp. salt
½ c. pecans, chopped
3 Tbs. butter

Directions:

1. Preheat oven to 325 degrees F.
2. In small bowl, combine huckleberries, sugar, lemon rind, and apples.
3. Mix well and place in a well buttered 8 x 8 x 2-inch baking pan.
4. In medium bowl, combine brown sugar, cinnamon, nutmeg, flour, oats, salt, and pecans.
5. Rub butter into the mixture with your fingers until it resembles coarse crumbs.
6. Spread evenly over the huckleberry filling.
7. Bake 45 minutes, or until the crust is brown.

Did You Know? . . . .

Did you know that bells summoning the faithful to worship was the first link to Christmas?

Christmas Delights Cookbook
A Collection of Christmas Recipes
Cookbook Delights Holiday Series Book 12

Dressings, Sauces, and Condiments

Table of Contents

Apple Cranberry Sauce

This is a delicious apple cranberry sauce for your holiday table.

Ingredients:

½ pkg. fresh or frozen cranberries (6 oz.)
4 lg. apples, cored, peeled, diced in chunks
½ c. water
1 c. sugar, or to taste depending on tartness of apples

Directions:

1. In medium saucepan, place all ingredients; bring to boil.
2. Simmer until apple chunks are just tender.
3. Sauce will thicken and color will blend as it cools.

Yields: 6 servings.

Apple-Poppy Seed Dressing

This is a flavorful salad dressing, a tasty combination with blended fresh apples. It is great served on your favorite greens or fruit.

Ingredients:

1 sm. fresh apple, peeled, cored, finely chopped
2 Tbs. lemon juice, fresh
½ c. sugar
½ c. lemon juice
2 tsp. onion, diced
1 tsp. prepared mustard, Dijon-style
½ tsp. salt
⅔ c. olive oil

174

1 Tbs. poppy seeds

Directions:

1. In small bowl, combine apple and lemon juice; set aside.
2. In blender or food processor, combine sugar, lemon juice, onion, mustard, and salt.
3. Process until well blended.
4. With machine still running, add oil in a slow steady stream until mixture is thick and smooth.
5. Add apple mixture and poppy seeds.
6. Blend just a few seconds more to mix.
7. Chill until ready to serve.

Balsamic Vinaigrette Dressing

My daughter, Marissa, loves balsamic vinegar, and this makes a tasty dressing.

Ingredients:

½ c. balsamic vinegar
1 Tbs. soy sauce
2 Tbs. honey
2 garlic cloves, minced
½ c. extra virgin olive oil
    crushed dried red pepper, to taste

Directions:

1. In medium bowl or food processor, whisk together balsamic vinegar, soy sauce, honey, garlic, and red pepper.
2. Add olive oil in a thin stream, whisking until emulsified.

Bourbon-Pineapple for Ham

This is a different twist for your holiday ham. A good sauce could not be easier to make than this.

Ingredients:

   1 c. bourbon
   1 c. pineapple juice

Directions:

   1. In small bowl, combine bourbon and pineapple juice.
   2. Mix well.
   3. Baste ham with this sauce continually throughout the roasting process.

Cherry Salad Dressing

The versatility of cherries is astounding. Throughout history they have been included in every sort of dish from soup to entrees to desserts. However, they are not limited to just those categories. Here, we employ fresh, sweet cherries to dress up a salad. Bursting with flavor, this exceptional salad dressing contains no oil, salt, or added sugar.

Ingredients:

   10 oz. fresh cherries, pitted
   ⅓ c. plus 1 Tbs. raspberry vinegar
   ½ c. water
   2 Tbs. vegetable seasoning, salt-free
   7 pitted dates, more or less to taste

Directions:

1. Place pitted cherries into a blender.
2. Add remaining ingredients and blend, starting on low speed for a few seconds.
3. Increase to high speed; blend until smooth and creamy.
4. Adjust the number of pitted dates to the sweetness of the cherries and to your taste.
5. Very sweet cherries may not need any sweetening at all, while tart cherries will need more dates.

Yields: 2 cups.

Christmas Relish

This is a delicious relish for your holiday table.

Ingredients:

1 pkg. frozen strawberries (10 oz.), sweetened, sliced, thawed
½ c. sugar
1 pkg. cranberries (12 oz.)

Directions:

1. Drain syrup from strawberries into 1-cup measure.
2. Add enough water to equal 1 cup liquid.
3. In 3-quart saucepan, over medium-high heat, heat syrup mixture, sugar, and cranberries, stirring occasionally.
4. Reduce heat to low; simmer, uncovered, for 10 minutes, or until cranberries have popped.
5. Stir in strawberries and cool to room temperature.
6. Spoon into a serving bowl, cover, and refrigerate 3 hours.

Cranberry Orange Relish

My mom used to make this for my dad. It is very good.

Ingredients:

    1½ lb. cranberries, raw
    3   c. sugar
    3   oranges, whole

Directions:

1. Wash, sort, and drain cranberries.
2. Cut oranges into quarters and remove seeds.
3. Put cranberries and oranges through food chopper.
4. Stir in sugar.
5. Store in refrigerator.

Yields: 50 servings (1½ tablespoons each).

Peppercorn-Raspberry Sauce

This colorful sauce will look beautiful on your holiday table, and you will especially enjoy this wonderful blend of flavors.

Ingredients:

    ½ c. dry white wine
    ¾ c. all-purpose broth or chicken broth
    2 Tbs. raspberry preserves or frozen raspberry sauce
    ½ c. whipping cream
    1 Tbs. butter
    2 Tbs. green peppercorns in water
      giblets from roasted duck or goose, drained, chopped

Directions:

1. Combine wine, broth, preserves, and giblets in saucepan; over medium heat, bring to boil.
2. Cook until liquid is reduced by half.
3. Add cream and continue to cook until liquid reduces enough to coat the back of a spoon.
4. Remove from heat and whisk in the butter.
5. Strain the sauce into a sauceboat and discard the giblets.
6. Stir in peppercorns and serve sauce with roasted bird.

Yields: 1½ cups.

Ranch Dressing

This gives a higher protein content ranch dressing, and it is still very tasty.

Ingredients:

2 c. cottage cheese
½ c. yogurt, drained
2 sm. garlic cloves, minced
1 tsp. dried oregano
1 tsp. dried thyme
2 tsp. parsley, fresh, chopped
½ c. buttermilk
2 Tbs. lemon juice
1 Tbs. red wine vinegar
white pepper, freshly ground

Directions:

1. Using a blender or food processor, combine all ingredients.
2. Blend until creamy and smooth.

Yields: 2½ cups.

Honey-Mustard Glaze

This is a delicious glaze for your holiday ham.

Ingredients:

    2 Tbs. prepared mustard
    1 c. brown sugar
    ½ c. honey
       pineapple rings
       maraschino cherries
       toothpicks

Directions:

1. Preheat oven to 300 degrees F.
2. In small bowl, combine first 3 ingredients.
3. Spread mixture over cooked ham.
4. Garnish with pineapple rings.
5. In the center of each ring, secure maraschino cherries with toothpicks.
6. Bake 30 minutes.

Hollandaise Sauce

This is a delicious sauce served over potatoes and other vegetables.

Ingredients:

    3 egg yolks
    ¼ lb. butter
    ½ c. white wine
    1 bay leaf
    4 pieces peppercorn
    1 Tbs. white vinegar
    1 Tbs. lemon juice
       salt and pepper, to taste

Directions:

1. In medium saucepan, over very low heat, add egg yolks and lemon juice stirring vigorously.
2. Add butter and white wine, stirring constantly with whisk until melted.
3. Add remaining ingredients and continue vigorous stirring until all butter is melted and sauce is thickened. (Be sure butter melts slowly so eggs have time to cook and thicken sauce without curdling.)
4. Keep warm in a double boiler over warm water (not hot water) until ready to serve.
5. Note: You may put hollandaise sauce in a small thermos to keep it warm.

Raspberry Vinaigrette

This only takes a minute to make, and you will enjoy this raspberry vinaigrette over salad greens.

Ingredients:

3 Tbs. raspberry jam, seedless
⅔ c. canola oil
⅓ c. red wine vinegar
¼ tsp. salt
¼ tsp. pepper

Directions:

1. Place jam in small microwave-safe bowl and microwave uncovered on high 10 to 15 seconds until melted.
2. Pour into a jar with tight-fitting lid. Add oil, vinegar, salt, and pepper; shake well, and serve.
3. Refrigerate any remaining vinaigrette.

Yields: ¾ cup.

Horseradish-Mustard Spread

This is so good on prime rib and on steak sandwiches.

Ingredients:

   3 Tbs. mayonnaise
   1 Tbs. fresh parsley, chopped
   1 Tbs. prepared horseradish
   1 Tbs. Dijon mustard
   2 tsp. garlic powder
   1 tsp. black pepper

Directions:

   1.   Combine all ingredients in small bowl; mix well.

Yields: ½ cup.

Raspberry Glaze

This is an ideal glaze with smoked meat - duck, pork, any game, chicken, turkey, or game hen.

Ingredients:

   1 Tbs. butter (for sautéing)
   2 Tbs. shallots, minced
   ½ oz. brandy
   2 oz. crème de cassis liqueur
   1 tsp. raspberry jelly or 1 tsp. sugar with ½ c. berries
   4 oz. veal stock (may substitute beef broth)
   2 oz. whole milk
      salt and pepper

Directions:

1. In large sauté pan, over medium-high heat, melt butter.
2. Add shallots and cook until light brown.
3. Add brandy, crème de cassis liqueur, and jelly (or sugar and raspberries).
4. Reduce until almost dry.
5. Add veal or beef stock and heat until reduced by half.
6. Remove from heat and swirl in milk.
7. Adjust seasoning with salt and pepper.
8. To serve, slice and arrange cooked meat on warm platter, and pour hot glaze over meat.
9. Serve immediately.

Tartar Sauce

You'll never buy tartar sauce from the store again after you taste this delicious, easy-to-make recipe.

Ingredients:

2 onion slices (⅛-inch), white or Spanish, diced
3 Tbs. capers, drained, patted dry, minced
1 Tbs. parsley, minced
1¼ c. mayonnaise
⅛ tsp. cayenne pepper, or to taste
¼ tsp. horseradish, or to taste

Directions:

1. In medium bowl, combine onion, capers, parsley, mayonnaise, cayenne pepper, and horseradish until well blended.
2. Cover; store in refrigerator until ready to use.

Yields: 1½ cups.

Russian Dressing

Try this Russian dressing for a zingy salad dressing.

Ingredients:

- 1 c. mayonnaise
- ¼ c. ketchup
- 1 Tbs. horseradish
- 1 tsp. onion, grated

Directions:

1. In small bowl, combine all ingredients.
2. Store in refrigerator in tightly sealed container.

Zucchini Relish

Zucchini relish is a very good replacement for sweet pickle relish to go with your holiday meals.

Ingredients:

- 2 c. zucchini (3 med.), chopped
- 1 c. onion (1 med.), chopped
- 2 Tbs. salt
- 4 c. water, cold, or enough to cover vegetables
- 1¾ c. sugar
- 1 c. cider vinegar
- 1 tsp. ground mustard

Directions:

1. In medium bowl, combine zucchini and onion.
2. Sprinkle with salt and cover with cold water.
3. Let stand 2 hours.
4. Drain, rinse, and drain again thoroughly.

5. In large saucepan, combine sugar, vinegar, and mustard; bring to boil.
6. Add vegetables; simmer 10 minutes.
7. Pack hot relish into hot jars, leaving ¼-inch headspace.
8. Adjust 2-piece lids.
9. Process 10 minutes in a boiling water canner.

Green Pesto Sauce

This is a delicious sauce that is so easy to make.

Ingredients:

2 c. fresh basil
2 med. garlic cloves
¼ tsp. salt
3 Tbs. pine nuts
½ c. olive oil
½ c. Parmesan, grated
2 Tbs. Romano, grated
2 Tbs. butter

Directions:

9. In food processor or blender, combine basil, garlic, salt, and pine nuts.
10. When evenly blended, with motor still running, add olive oil in slow, steady stream. Turn motor off.
11. Scrape bowl to blend to smooth consistency.
12. Add cheese and softened butter; process briefly.
13. Genuine pesto is always made with fresh basil. If unavailable you may make a substitute sauce using 1 cup fresh spinach leaves, ½ cup coarsely chopped Italian parsley, and 2 tablespoons dried basil leaves.

Yields: 2 servings.

Red Marinara Sauce

This is one of our favorite sauces.

Ingredients:

1 Tbs. safflower oil
1 Tbs. olive oil
1 Tbs. butter
1 sm. onion, chopped
2 garlic cloves, minced
¾ lb. mushrooms, sliced
1 med. carrot, grated
1 celery stalk, finely chopped
2 Tbs. green pepper, finely chopped
2 Tbs. fresh parsley, chopped
1 bay leaf
1 tsp. dried oregano
½ tsp. dried thyme
½ tsp. dried basil
¼ tsp. pepper
3 c. tomatoes (28 oz.), cut into quarters
⅔ c. tomato paste (6 oz.)
   pepper, to taste

Directions:

1. In large saucepan, heat safflower oil, olive oil, and butter.
2. Stir in onion, garlic, and mushrooms; sauté until softened.
3. Add carrot, celery, green pepper, parsley, bay leaf, oregano, thyme, basil, pepper, and cayenne pepper.
4. Cover, reduce heat, and simmer 30 minutes.
5. Remove bay leaf.
6. Note: This sauce becomes tastier with time.
7. If possible, make a day or two in advance and refrigerate until ready to use.

Christmas Delights Cookbook
A Collection of Christmas Recipes
Cookbook Delights Holiday Series Book 12

Jams, Jellies, and Syrups

Table of Contents

Page

A Basic Guide for Canning Jams, Jellies, and Syrups

1. Wash jars in hot, soapy water inside and out with brush or soft cloth.
2. Run your finger around rim of each jar, discarding any with cracks or chips.
3. Rinse well in clean, clear, hot water, using tongs to avoid burns to hands or fingers.
4. Place upside down on clean cloth to drain well.
5. Place lids in boiling water for 2 minutes to sterilize and keep hot until placing on rim of jar.
6. Immediately prior to filling each jar, immerse in very hot water with tongs to heat jar (avoids breakage of jar with hot liquid).
7. Fill jar to within 1 inch of top of rim or to level recommended in recipe.
8. Wipe rim with clean damp cloth to remove any particles of food, and check again for any chips or cracks.
9. With tongs, place lid from hot bath directly onto rim of jar.
10. Using gloves, cloth, or holders, tighten lid firmly onto jar with ring or use single formed lid in place of ring to cover inner lid. Do not tighten down too hard as it may impede sealing.
11. Place on protected surface to cool, taking care to not disturb lid and ring. A slight indentation of lid will be apparent when sealed.
12. Leave overnight until thoroughly cooled.
13. When cooled, wipe jars with damp cloth and then label and date each.
14. Store upright on shelf in cool, dark place.

Raspberry Freezer Jam

This raspberry freezer jam tastes like you just made it today. It is so delicious; we put it on toast and muffins, on cake, ice cream, yogurt, pancakes, and waffles.

Ingredients:

2 c. raspberries, crushed (2-3 pt.)
4 c. sugar
1 pouch liquid pectin

Directions:

1. Wash and rinse 4 pint jars.
2. Wash, thoroughly drain, and crush raspberries, one layer at a time.
3. Sieve part of pulp to remove seeds, if desired.
4. Measure 2 cups prepared raspberries and sugar into large bowl.
5. Mix well and let stand 10 minutes.
6. Stir in liquid pectin and continue stirring 3 minutes.
7. Ladle jam into clean pint jar to within ½-inch of top rim.
8. Using nonmetallic utensil, remove air bubbles.
9. Wipe jar rim removing any stickiness.
10. Cover with lids. Repeat for remaining jam.
11. Let stand in refrigerator until set.
12. Freeze within 24 hours for long term storage.
13. Store in freezer up to 1 year or in refrigerator up to 3 weeks.

Yields: 4 pint jars.

Did You Know? . . . .

Did you know the most precious gift you can receive is sharing with someone the gift of giving?

Apple Cider Jelly

This is great tasting jelly made from just one ingredient. The flavor is dependent on the quality and flavor of the apple cider. It is great on toast or muffins or anything you choose.

Ingredients:

2 qt. apple cider

Directions:

1. Heat cider in heavy saucepan over moderate heat, and bring to simmer.
2. Boil 45 to 60 minutes to jelling point of 220 degrees F.
3. Remove from heat; cool.
4. Store chilled in refrigerator for up to 4 to 6 weeks.
5. Serve slightly chilled or at room temperature.

Apple Ginger Jam

When you add ginger to apple jam, it livens up the taste. Essence of ginger is a natural extract of ginger, and can be found in a health food store or natural food market.

Ingredients:

4 lb. green apples
4 lb. sugar
1 qt. water
2 oz. essence of ginger

Directions:

1. Pare and core apples, and cut them into shapes as much like gingerroot as possible.

2. In large pot, boil sugar with water for 30 minutes, or until you have syrup.
3. Keep syrup boiling quickly while you add the apples; add at least 2 ounces of essence of ginger.
4. Remove from heat and stir as little as possible.
5. The mixture will take about 1 hour to clear and become yellow.
6. Strain the apples out and discard.
7. Skim foam from the surface and follow standard directions for canning jams and jellies found on page 188.

Cherry and Raspberry Jam

This is a delicious jam and is good on everything from toast to biscuits.

Ingredients:

1 qt. sweet cherries, pitted, chopped
¼ c. orange juice
2 Tbs. lemon rind
1 Tbs. orange peel, grated
1½ qt. raspberries
1 qt. sugar (4 c.)

Directions:

1. In large pot, add cherries, orange juice, lemon rind, and orange peel; bring to boil.
2. Cook 10 minutes, stirring frequently.
3. Add raspberries and sugar.
4. Bring to boil, stirring frequently.
5. Boil 15 minutes, to jam stage.
6. Remove from heat, stir, and skim for 5 minutes.
7. Pour into hot, sterile jars, and seal.

Bing Cherry Sauce

Bing cherries are excellent and make this sauce extra delicious.

Ingredients:

¾ c. sugar
¼ tsp. salt
3 Tbs. cornstarch
¾ c. cherry juice
1 Tbs. butter
2 Tbs. lemon juice
2 c. sour red or Bing cherries, canned or frozen

Directions:

1. In large saucepan, combine sugar, salt, and cornstarch; stir in juice.
2. Cook until thickened, stirring constantly.
3. Stir in remaining ingredients.
4. Serve over cheesecake or ice cream.

Berry Jelly

This combination of berries makes a delightful berry jelly. It also makes great gifts.

Ingredients:

1   lb. blackberry juice (2 c.)
1   lb. boysenberry juice (2 c.)
1   lb. dewberry juice (2 c.)
1   lb. youngberry juice (2 c.)
3½ c. fruit juice
1   pkg. powdered pectin
2   Tbs. lemon juice
5   c. sugar

Directions:

1. In large saucepan, combine fruit juice, pectin, and lemon juice.
2. Over high heat, bring to boil.
3. Add sugar, stirring until dissolved.
4. Return to rolling boil; boil hard for 1 minute, stirring constantly.
5. Remove from heat; skim foam if necessary.
6. Ladle hot jelly into hot, sterilized jars, leaving ¼-inch headspace.
7. Adjust 2-piece caps.
8. Process 5 minutes in a boiling water canner.

Huckleberry-Orange Jelly

This is a simple-to-make huckleberry-orange jelly.

Ingredients:

3 c. huckleberry juice
1 c. orange juice
6 c. sugar
2 pkg. liquid fruit pectin

Directions:

1. In large saucepan, combine huckleberry juice, orange juice, and sugar.
2. Over medium-high heat, bring mixture to rolling boil, stirring constantly.
3. Add liquid fruit pectin, stirring quickly into fruit juice mixture.
4. Return to rolling boil and boil 1 minute, stirring constantly.
5. Remove from heat, skim off foam, and ladle into hot, sterilized jars.

Yields: 7 to 8 half-pints.

Instant Raspberry Cordial Jam

This is so quick and easy to make, and the flavor is wonderful.

Ingredients:

  12 oz. raspberry jam
  1-2 Tbs. Chambord or other raspberry liqueur

Directions:

  1. Stir liqueur into jam and cover.
  2. Refrigerate at least 1 day to allow flavors to meld.

Blackberry Jam

This makes a delicious blackberry jam.

Ingredients:

  5½ c. blackberries, fresh or frozen
  7   c. sugar
  1   pkg. powdered fruit pectin

Directions:

  1. Rinse and remove stems and hulls from berries and thoroughly crush, removing seeds from half of the berries by sieving.
  2. Place berries in 6 to 8-quart saucepan (preferably stainless steel; stir in fruit pectin.
  3. Bring fruit and pectin mixture to full boil, stirring constantly.
  4. Remove from heat; stir in sugar completely to prevent burning and sticking to the pan.

5. Return to heat; return to full rolling boil for 1
   minute, stirring constantly, then remove from heat.
6. Skim foam from surface.
7. Follow standard directions for canning jams and
   jellies found on page 188.

Yields: 8 cups.

Cherry Raspberry Sauce

*Here is another great sauce for serving over your
favorite dessert.*

Ingredients:

   3 c. fresh sweet cherries, pitted
   2 c. raspberries, fresh or frozen, divided
   ⅓ c. sugar
   1 Tbs. lemon juice
   ½ tsp. almond extract
   ¼ tsp. ground cinnamon

Directions:

1. In medium saucepan, combine cherries, 1 cup
   raspberries, sugar, and lemon juice.
2. Place over medium heat, stirring to dissolve the
   sugar.
3. Bring to boil, reduce heat slightly, and cook at a low
   boil for 15 minutes, stirring often.
4. Transfer to a bowl.
5. Stir in remaining raspberries, almond extract, and
   cinnamon.
6. Cool.
7. Serve over vanilla ice cream, plain cheesecake, or
   angel food cake.

Cherry Syrup

This is not only delicious, but the color of this syrup decorates your table with holiday red.

Ingredients:

    4   lb. cherries, frozen or fresh
    ¼-½ c. sugar
    1   Tbs. cornstarch
           peel of 1 lemon (all in 1 piece)
           juice of 1 lemon

Directions:

1. Thaw and drain frozen cherries.
2. Remove cherry pits.
3. Place cherries, lemon peel, lemon juice, and sugar in a saucepan with a little water.
4. Bring slowly to a boil.
5. Cook until color changes.
6. While cooking, adjust lemon juice or sugar to taste.
7. Remove lemon peel.
8. Thicken with cornstarch.
9. Serve over ice cream or with Christmas pudding.

Currant Jelly

You can use red currants or black currants for this jelly, or a combination of both.

Ingredients:

    6½ c. currant juice
    1   pkg. powdered pectin
    7   c. sugar

Directions:

1. In large saucepan, combine currant juice with pectin.
2. Over high heat, bring to boil.
3. Add sugar, stirring until dissolved.
4. Return to rolling boil.
5. Boil hard for 1 minute, stirring constantly.
6. Remove from heat.
7. Skim foam from surface.
8. Follow standard directions for canning jams and jellies found on page 188.

Quick Raspberry Jelly

This jelly is quick to make because it uses already prepared juice, but it is still delicious and will get you out of the kitchen in a jiffy.

Ingredients:

2 cans raspberry juice (10 oz. ea.)
¾ c. water
2 c. sugar
1 bottle liquid pectin (6 oz.)
5 half-pt. jars

Directions:

1. In heavy saucepan, combine raspberry juice, water, and sugar.
2. Over high heat, bring to boil, stirring constantly.
3. Stir in pectin and quickly bring to full rolling boil. Liquid will continue to boil when stirred.
4. Boil 1 minute.
5. Remove from heat, skim off foam, pour into jars, and seal.

Rhubarb-Pineapple Jam

This is an easy-to-make, rhubarb-pineapple jam.

Ingredients:

5 c. rhubarb, fresh or frozen, chopped
4 c. sugar
1 can pineapple, crushed (20 oz.), drained
1 pkg. strawberry flavored gelatin (6 oz.)

Directions:

1. In large saucepan or stock pot, combine rhubarb, sugar, and pineapple.
2. Over medium-high heat, bring to boil.
3. Boil for 10 minutes, stirring frequently.
4. Jars can be sterilized at the same time.
5. After rhubarb mixture has boiled 10 minutes, remove from heat.
6. Stir in strawberry flavored gelatin powder.
7. Transfer to sterile jars and seal.
8. Allow jars to cool in a draft-free area.
9. Refrigerate jars after seal has been broken.

Sparkling Holiday Jam

This makes a great holiday red jam full of flavor and texture.

Ingredients:

2½ qt. strawberries, coarsely chopped
1   pkg. cranberries (12 oz.), fresh or frozen, chopped
2   pkg. powdered fruit pectin (2 oz. ea.)
1   tsp. butter
5   lb. sugar

Directions:

1. Sterilize jars and lids in boiling water for at least 10 minutes.
2. Let simmer while making jam.
3. In large saucepan, combine strawberries, cranberries, pectin, and butter.
4. Bring to boil; stir in sugar, and return to boil.
5. Cook 1 minute; remove from heat.
6. Quickly fill jars to within ½-inch from top.
7. Wipe rims clean and put on lids.

Easy Huckleberry Jam

This is an easy-to-make jam for all your seasonal huckleberries.

Ingredients:

1 qt. huckleberries (5½ c.)
7 c. sugar
1 pkg. less 1 Tbs. powdered fruit pectin

Directions:

1. Wash berries and thoroughly crush, removing seeds from half the berries by sieving.
2. Place berries in 6 to 8-quart saucepan, and stir in fruit pectin.
3. Bring fruit and pectin mixture to full boil, stirring constantly.
4. Remove from heat; add sugar, mixing in thoroughly to prevent burning and sticking to pan.
5. Return to heat.
6. Stirring constantly, return to full rolling boil.
7. Boil 1 minute; remove from heat.
8. Skim foam from the surface and ladle into hot, sterilized jars. Seal at once.

Yields: 8 cups.

Cranberry Jelly

Cranberry jelly is a refreshing and colorful addition to your Christmas table. It also makes a great holiday gift.

Ingredients:

    2 c. fresh cranberries
    1 c. apple juice, concentrated
    ¼ c. lemon juice
    3 oz. liquid pectin
    5 Tbs. glycerin
    1 Tbs. gelatin, unflavored

Directions:

1. Wash and pick over cranberries, discarding any that are soft.
2. Place in a deep saucepan, add fruit juices.
3. Cover and simmer 20 minutes, until fruit is soft.
4. Mash to break up any berries left whole.
5. Strain through food mill to remove seeds.
6. Return to saucepan, heat to boiling.
7. Add pectin, glycerin, and gelatin, stirring well.
8. Boil 1 minute; remove from heat.
9. Skim foam from the surface.
10. Follow standard directions for canning jams and jellies found on page 188.

Did You Know? . . . .

Did you know that one of the greatest joys you will ever feel is the look in your child's eyes when he gives a plate of cookies you have made together to a neighbor or friend, or a stranger?

Christmas Delights Cookbook

A Collection of Christmas Recipes
Cookbook Delights Holiday Series Book 12

Main Dishes

Table of Contents

Page

Baked Rigatoni, Sausage, and Noodles

This is an easy-to-make, casserole-style dish. Our family loves rigatoni noodles, and the addition of sausage and cheese makes it very tasty. For vegetarians, substitute with mushrooms or broccoli for the sausage.

Ingredients:

- 6   c. rigatoni noodles, uncooked
- 1   lb. rope-style hot or sweet Italian sausage
- ½   c. onion, chopped
- 1¾ c. ricotta cheese
- 3   c. spaghetti sauce
- 1½ c. mozzarella cheese, shredded
- ½   c. Parmesan cheese, freshly grated, plus extra to sprinkle on top

Directions:

1. Preheat oven to 400 degrees F.
2. Cook pasta according to package directions, drain.
3. In 5-quart saucepan, over medium heat, cook meat until brown on both sides.
4. Remove from pan; slice into thin pieces.
5. Return meat to pan with onion, cook 5 minutes until onion is tender and meat is thoroughly cooked.
6. Stir in hot pasta and ricotta cheese until well blended.
7. In 9 x 13-inch baking dish, spread 1 cup spaghetti sauce.
8. Spoon pasta mixture over sauce.
9. Spread remaining spaghetti sauce evenly over pasta; sprinkle with remaining cheeses.
10. Cover with foil.
11. Bake 20 minutes.
12. Remove foil.
13. Bake 5 minutes, or until hot and bubbly.

Grilled Game Hens with Raspberry

If you are looking for something different for your holiday gathering, the raspberry marinade in this recipe is wonderful.

Ingredients:

- 6 Cornish game hens, split in half
- 3 c. raspberries, fresh or frozen
- 1 c. raspberry vinegar
- ¾ c. olive oil
- 2 bay leaves
- 1 Tbs. dried thyme
  salt and pepper, to taste

Directions:

1. One day before serving, rinse birds, pat dry, and place on shallow baking dish.
2. Combine raspberries and vinegar in saucepan.
3. Boil 1 minute.
4. Remove from heat.
5. Stir in oil, bay leaves, and thyme.
6. Cool to room temperature.
7. Pour the marinade over birds.
8. Sprinkle with salt and pepper.
9. Marinate overnight in refrigerator, turning occasionally.
10. Prepare hot coals for grilling.
11. Remove birds from the marinade, and grill a few inches above hot coals, basting occasionally with the marinade, until juices run clear when the thickest part of a thigh is pierced.
12. Serve immediately.

Baked Salmon with Dill Mustard

Baked salmon is so easy to make and so delicious. The dill mustard sauce really complements the delicate flavor of the salmon.

Ingredients for dill mustard sauce:

    ½ c. mayonnaise
    ½ c. sour cream
    3 Tbs. parsley leaves, fresh, minced
    2 Tbs. mustard, Dijon style
    2 Tbs. dill weed, fresh, minced
    2 tsp. lemon juice, freshly squeezed
       salt and freshly ground pepper, to taste

Ingredients for salmon:

    2-3 lb. salmon fillet 1½-inch thick
    3 Tbs. extra virgin olive oil
       coarse kosher salt
       freshly ground black pepper

Directions for dill mustard sauce:

1. In small bowl, mix together mayonnaise, sour cream, parsley, Dijon mustard, dill weed, lemon juice, salt, and pepper.
2. Cover bowl with plastic wrap and refrigerate for at least 3 hours before serving.

Directions for salmon:

1. Preheat oven to 350 degrees F.
2. Line the bottom of an ungreased broiling pan with aluminum foil and spray broiler rack with canola cooking spray.
3. Wash salmon, pat dry, rub with olive oil, and sprinkle with coarse salt and pepper.
4. Place salmon skin side down onto rack.
5. Bake salmon uncovered for 8 to 12 minutes, or until a meat thermometer registers an internal temperature of 140 degrees F.

6. Salmon will be slightly opaque in the thickest part.
7. Note: When the salmon is removed from the oven, it continues to cook and the juices redistribute. The meat temperature will rise 5 to 10 degrees during this time.
8. Carefully remove salmon from pan and transfer onto individual serving plates.
9. Serve with the cold mustard dill sauce.
10. Approximate cooking times for salmon:
    - ¼ to ⅓-inch: 3 to 4 minutes
    - ½ to ¾-inch: 4 to 6 minutes
    - 1 to 1½-inch: 8 to 12 minutes

Yields: 4 to 6 servings.

King Crab Legs with Butter

These crab legs are pre-cooked and flash frozen.

Ingredients:

1 lg. pot of water
½ c. sugar
½ c. butter, melted for serving
   king crab legs

Directions:

1. Bring water to a boil in a large pot.
2. Place frozen legs in pot, submerging all legs.
3. Reduce heat to lowest setting.
4. Cover pot, do not allow to boil.
5. Crab is ready to serve in 20 minutes.
6. Tip: Break legs into smaller sections if pot is not large enough to hold full leg.
7. Alternate cooking method: If you do not have a large pot, place legs on baking sheet and add at least 1 inch of water.
8. Cover tight with tinfoil. Put in a preheated oven at 325 degrees F. for 30 minutes.
9. Serve with warm melted butter.
10. Try adding garlic or other herbs.

Grilled Honey Dijon Turkey Breast

If you like turkey, you will love this.

Ingredients for turkey preparation:

¼ c. kosher salt
¼ c. sugar
2 Tbs. black pepper, ground
1 Tbs. cinnamon
2 Tbs. ginger, minced
4 c. water, cold, divided
1 turkey breast, boneless, skinless, cut in half
3-4 garlic cloves, minced

Ingredients for honey Dijon glaze:

3 Tbs. honey
2 Tbs. Dijon mustard
1 chipotle chili in adobo, minced
2 tsp. balsamic vinegar

Directions for turkey and marinade preparation:

1. In large saucepan, combine salt, sugar, pepper, cinnamon, and ginger along with 1 cup water in large saucepan.
2. Bring to boil, reduce heat; add 3 cups water.
3. Place turkey in resealable container, or plastic bag, add minced garlic and brine.
4. Seal and allow to rest in refrigerator up to 24 hours.

Directions for grilling turkey with honey Dijon glaze:

1. Preheat grill to medium heat.
2. Combine honey, chipotle, mustard, vinegar in bowl.
3. Remove turkey from refrigerator; discard brine mix.

4. Place turkey on grill rack; cook 25 to 30 minutes, turning once.
5. Baste with honey Dijon glaze during cooking.
6. Turkey should be between 165 to 170 degrees F. when done.
7. Remove from heat; let rest 5 to 10 minutes before slicing.

Grilled Turkey with Raspberry

This is great to make for a smaller holiday gathering. Your guests will enjoy this.

Ingredients:

4 lb. turkey breast (1 lg. breast) skinned, quartered
½ c. raspberry vinegar
2 Tbs. shallots, minced
½ c. yogurt, nonfat, plain
1 tsp. curry powder

Directions:

1. Place turkey breast quarters into large, shallow pan.
2. In small bowl, combine vinegar and shallots and pour over turkey.
3. Cover with plastic wrap; marinate 8 to 10 hours in refrigerator.
4. Combine yogurt and curry powder; set aside.
5. Prepare coals for grilling.
6. Wrap turkey breasts in aluminum foil and place on grill.
7. Cook 20 minutes; unwrap, grill 5 minutes more, turning once to brown lightly.
8. Spoon marinade over turkey frequently during last 5 minutes of grilling.
9. Serve with curried yogurt as a spicy sauce.

Ham Casserole Supreme

This is a very easy-to-make macaroni and cheese casserole.

Ingredients:

1½ lb. cooked ham, cubed
½ c. onions, chopped
1   lb. Cheddar cheese, cubed
6   eggs, hard-boiled, chopped
2   cans mushrooms, drained
¼ c. green peppers, chopped
¼ c. pimento, chopped
2   Tbs. prepared mustard
2   cans cream of mushroom soup concentrate
1   qt. milk
1½ c. water
14 oz. macaroni, uncooked
1   c. cracker crumbs

Directions:

1. Preheat oven to 350 degrees F.
2. In large bowl, combine ham, onions, cheese, eggs, mushrooms, green peppers, pimento, and mustard.
3. In small bowl, combine soup, milk, and water.
4. Spread macaroni evenly in 9 x 13-inch baking pan.
5. Add ham and cheese mixture; stir soup mixture into pan.
6. Top casserole with cracker crumbs.
7. Bake 40 minutes, or until hot and bubbly.

Did You Know? . . .

Did you know the top selling Christmas trees are: balsam fir, Douglas fir, Fraser fir, noble fir, Scotch pine, Virginia pine, and white pine?

Ham and Cheese Casserole

This is an easy-to-make casserole that is tasty and uses ingredients that most of us have on hand. This is great for a busy day.

Ingredients:

2   c. butter, divided
½   c. flour
½   tsp. salt
¼   tsp. pepper
1   tsp. dry mustard
1   tsp. hot sauce
3   c. milk, scalded
¼   c. onion, minced
1   c. sharp Cheddar cheese
1   pkg. frozen mixed vegetables (16 oz.), thawed
1   lb. cooked ham, cut in 1½-inch strips
1½ c. fresh bread cubes

Directions:

1. Preheat oven to 350 degrees F.
2. Melt 1½ cups of butter in large kettle.
3. Stir in flour, salt, pepper, mustard, and hot sauce.
4. Gradually stir in scalded milk.
5. Cook 15 minutes, stirring until smooth and thick.
6. Add onions and cheese.
7. Cook, stirring until cheese melts.
8. Stir in thawed vegetables and ham strips.
9. Spoon into 9 x 13-inch baking pan.
10. Melt remaining butter, and then pour over bread cubes.
11. Mix well.
12. Sprinkle bread cubes evenly over top.
13. Bake 1 hour, or until bubbly.

Ham Loaf

This is an easy-to-make dinner, great for those evenings in which you are too busy to spend much time preparing a meal.

Ingredients:

    2 c. soft bread crumbs
    1 c. milk
    2 eggs, slightly beaten
    2 lb. ham, ground
    1 lb. ground beef
    ¼ tsp. salt
    ¼ tsp. pepper
    ½ c. brown sugar, packed
    1 Tbs. prepared mustard

Directions:

1. Preheat oven to 325 degrees F.
2. In large bowl, soak bread crumbs in milk; add eggs.
3. In another bowl, combine ham, beef, salt, and pepper.
4. Combine with bread mixture; mix lightly.
5. Pack into a 9 x 5-inch loaf pan.
6. Bake 1 hour; drain off fat.
7. In small bowl, combine brown sugar and mustard; spread over top of loaf.
8. Continue baking about 45 minutes.
9. Note: You may prepare 24 hours ahead and leave in the refrigerator until ready to bake.

Did You Know? . . .

Did you know that our custom of kissing under the mistletoe came from the beliefs of the Scandinavians that holly was a symbol of peace?

Sauerbraten

My husband lived in Germany and actually has some German heritage, so I try to share these traditions with our blended family. This is a delicious way to prepare your beef roast for a Sunday supper.

Ingredients:

- 4 lb. boneless chuck or rump roast
- 2 c. wine vinegar
- 2 c. water
- 1 garlic clove
- ¾ c. onion, sliced
- 1 bay leaf
- 10 peppercorns
- ¼ c. sugar
- 3 whole cloves
- 2 Tbs. bacon drippings
- 1½ c. sour cream
- salt and pepper, to taste
- flour

Directions:

1. In large bowl, season meat with salt, pepper.
2. In small saucepan, bring vinegar and water to boil.
3. Add garlic, onion, bay leaf, peppercorns, sugar, and cloves.
4. Pour marinade over beef, cover, and refrigerate 12 hours or overnight.
5. Remove meat and dry thoroughly with paper towels; reserve marinade.
6. Dredge meat with flour.
7. In heavy skillet, heat bacon drippings and add meat.
8. Brown on all sides.
9. Add 2 cups of marinade; cover tightly, and simmer gently until meat is tender, 2½ to 3 hours.
10. Remove meat to warm platter; slice, and keep hot.
11. Thicken gravy with a little flour mixed with water.
12. Stir in sour cream and serve gravy over sliced meat.

Smoked Beer Can Turkey

Double the size of the can for this big bird and you can smoke a turkey on a beer can. This is a great way to keep the turkey moist by putting steam inside the turkey while it cooks.

Ingredients:

1   whole turkey, about 15 lb.
12 oz. beer plus 2 Tbs.
6   bay leaves
2   tsp. thyme
4   Tbs. brown sugar, divided
2   Tbs. paprika
1   Tbs. salt
1   Tbs. black pepper
1   tsp. cayenne pepper
2   Tbs. ketchup
2   Tbs. white vinegar
2   tsp. hot sauce
1   empty beer can (24 oz.)

Directions for beer can and beer:

1. Empty beer into another container.
2. Cut top of can off and pour in 12 ounces beer.
3. Add bay leaves and thyme; set aside.

Directions for turkey rub:

1. Combine 2 tablespoons brown sugar with paprika, salt, and both peppers.

Directions for turkey baste:

1. In another container combine remaining brown sugar, ketchup, vinegar, 2 tablespoons beer, and hot sauce.

Directions for cooking turkey:

1. Prepare smoker for 6-hour smoke.
2. Rub surface of turkey with the spice rub. Get as much as you can under the skin, particularly over the breast meat.
3. Stand beer can up on the smoker grate and gently set turkey over can so the can is completely inside the cavity of the turkey.
4. Make sure the turkey stands easily and doesn't sway. Turkey needs to be stable.
5. Once you have the turkey in the smoker, let it cook for about 6 hours at 250 degrees F.
6. Turkey is done when internal temperature in the thigh reaches 165 degrees F.
7. Baste turkey with baste mixture every 2 hours.

Perfect Prime Rib

When following these directions you can't help but have a roast that is delectable. Enjoy.

Ingredients:

7 lb. standing prime rib roast, loin end, tied

Directions:

1. Preheat oven to 325 degrees F.
2. Heat a large roasting pan over two burners at medium-high heat.
3. Place roast in hot pan; cook 6 to 8 minutes until browned on all sides.
4. Remove roast from pan.
5. Set wire rack in pan and set roast on rack.
6. Season generously with salt and pepper, to taste.
7. Place roast on lower rack of oven, and roast about 3½ hours (about 30 minutes per pound), or until a meat thermometer reads 130 degrees F.
8. Let stand 20 minutes before slicing.

Yields: 8 to 12 servings.

White Mizithra on Bow Ties

This dish is always enjoyable.

Ingredients:

　　1 c. butter, unsalted
　　1 pinch salt
　　1 pinch white pepper
　　1 dash lemon juice
　　2 c. baby spinach leaves
　　1 oz. fresh basil leaves, torn
　　1 tsp. garlic, minced
　　2 lb. bow ties, cooked, drained
　　1 c. mizithra cheese, shredded
　　1 sprig of parsley
　　2 Tbs. red bell pepper, roasted, diced

Directions:

1. Add butter to a hot sauté pan, and heat until it begins to brown.
2. Add salt, pepper, and a dash of lemon juice just before butter starts to burn.
3. Add spinach, basil, garlic, and bow ties; toss well.
4. Add cheese; toss well until the bow ties are evenly coated with the cheese.
5. Gently spoon into a serving bowl with a slotted spoon to prevent an excess of liquid.
6. Garnish with the parsley and red peppers.

Ham and Cheese Tortilla

This is an easy sandwich for a busy person on the go.

Ingredients:

1 whole wheat tortilla (9-inch)

1 oz. ham
1 oz. provolone cheese

Directions:

1. Place tortilla on the toaster tray and top with ham and cheese.
2. Toast on medium, or until cheese is lightly melted.
3. Remove from toaster oven; fold in half, and enjoy.
4. If using microwave, cook on high 30 to 45 seconds, or until cheese is melted.

Yields: 1 serving.

Turkey Thawing Methods

The experts recommend refrigerator thawing. However, if you are short on time and need a quicker method for thawing, try one of these.

1. Thawing turkey at room temperature allows bacterial growth and is not recommended.
2. To thaw a turkey in the refrigerator, thaw breast side up in its unopened wrapper on a tray in the refrigerator.
3. Allow at least one day of thawing for every four pounds of turkey and be sure to drain the juices off the tray before they overflow.
4. To cold-thaw the turkey, thaw breast side down in its unopened wrapper in cold water to cover.
5. Change water every 30 minutes to keep surface cold.
6. Estimate minimum thawing time to be 30 minutes per pound for whole turkey.
7. Neck and giblets in plastic bags allow easy removal. Unique leg tuck eliminates trussing.

Turkey and Dumplings

This is a delicious way to eat turkey, or even turkey leftovers…one of our favorites.

Ingredients:

3½ lb. assorted turkey pieces
8   c. turkey broth
2   c. flour
1   Tbs. baking powder
½   tsp. salt
½   c. butter, cold
½   c. water

Directions:

1. In large, wide pot, simmer turkey pieces in the broth until turkey is tender, 30 minutes or more.
2. Remove turkey and set aside.
3. When cool enough to handle, skin and bone the turkey and shred or cut into bite-size pieces.
4. If desired, skim turkey fat off surface of the broth.
5. In large bowl, mix flour, baking powder, and salt.
6. Using food processor or 2 knives, cut butter into flour mixture until it is the size of very small peas, and distributed throughout dry ingredients.
7. Add water and knead 8 to 10 times.
8. If the dough seems too sticky, add more flour.
9. Roll dough to ⅛-inch thick; cut into 1-inch squares.
10. Bring broth to rolling boil, drop in dumplings, cover pot, and reduce heat to simmer.
11. Cook 10 minutes, or until dumplings are cooked.
12. Overcooking will cause the dumplings to fall apart.
13. To serve, place turkey pieces in a bowl, and ladle hot broth and dumplings over the turkey.

Christmas Delights Cookbook
A Collection of Christmas Recipes
Cookbook Delights Holiday Series Book 12

Pies

Table of Contents

A Basic Recipe for Pie Crust

This is a very good recipe for a delicious, flaky crust.

Ingredients for single crust:

1½ c. sifted flour
½   tsp. salt
½   c. shortening
4-5 Tbs. ice water

Ingredients for double crust:

2   c. sifted flour
1   tsp. salt
⅔   c. shortening
5-7 Tbs. ice water

Directions for single crust:

1. In large bowl stir together flour and salt.
2. Cut in shortening with pastry blender or mix with fingertips until pieces are size of coarse crumbs.
3. Sprinkle 2 tablespoons ice water over flour mixture, tossing with fork.
4. Add just enough remaining water 1 tablespoon at a time to moisten dough, tossing so dough holds together.
5. Roll pastry into 11-inch circle, and wrap in plastic wrap; refrigerate for 1 hour.
6. Preheat oven to 425 degrees F.
7. Remove plastic wrap from pastry, and fit pastry into 9-inch pie plate.
8. Fold edge under and then crimp between thumb and forefinger to make fluted crust.
9. For filled pie with an instant or cooked filling (cream-filled, custard-filled, etc.), prick crust all over with fork then bake 15 to 20 minutes until done.
10. If preparing pie with uncooked filling (such as pumpkin), do not prick crust; pour filling into unbaked pastry shell, and then bake as directed.

Directions for double crust:

1. Turn desired filling into pastry-lined pie plate; trim overhanging edge of pastry ½ inch from rim of plate.
2. Cut slits with knife in top crust for steam vents.
3. Place over filling; trim overhanging edge of pastry 1 inch from rim of plate.
4. Fold and roll top edge under lower edge, pressing on rim to seal; flute.
5. Cover fluted edge with 2- to 3-inch-wide strip of aluminum foil to prevent excessive browning.
6. Remove foil during last 15 minutes of baking.

Yields: 1 pie crust (9-inch single or double).

A Basic Cookie or Graham Cracker Crust

This is a great crust for use with cream pies or for an unbaked pie. Use your favorite flavor of cookie to complement your filling, or use graham crackers.

Ingredients:

  2 c. cookie or graham cracker crumbs, finely crushed
  ⅓ c. sugar
  ½ c. butter, melted

Directions:

1. Combine crumbs, sugar, and butter.
2. Press mixture firmly against bottom and up sides of 9-inch pie plate.
3. Baking is not necessary, but if preferred crust may be baked at 400 degrees F. for 10 minutes.

Yields: 1 pie crust (9-inch).

Banana Cream Pie

My son Kyler and daughter Kelsey particularly enjoy this pie and so would your guests. This recipe has more bananas and pudding for an extra flavor.

Ingredients:

¾ c. sugar
½ c. flour
¼ tsp. salt
3 c. whole milk
3 egg yolks, beaten
3 Tbs. butter
1¼ tsp. vanilla extract
1 pie crust (9-inch), baked
5 bananas, sliced

Directions:

1. Preheat oven to 350 degrees F.
2. In medium saucepan, combine sugar, flour, and salt.
3. Add milk gradually while stirring gently.
4. Cook over medium heat, stirring constantly, until the mixture is bubbly.
5. Keep stirring, and cook 2 more minutes, then remove from burner.
6. Stir a small quantity of the hot mixture into the beaten egg yolks, and immediately add egg yolk mixture to the rest of the hot mixture.
7. Cook for 3 more minutes. Remember to keep stirring so you don't burn the pudding.
8. Remove mixture from stove; add butter and vanilla.
9. Stir until a smooth consistency.
10. Slice bananas into the cooled baked pastry shell.
11. Top with pudding mixture.
12. Bake 12 to 15 minutes.
13. Chill for 1 hour.

Caramel Pecan Pie

This is a very easy-to-make pie with the delicious taste of caramel and pecan.

Ingredients for pie:

 1 can sweetened condensed milk (14 oz.)
 1 c. pecans, chopped
 ½ c. brown sugar, packed
 1 toasty oat crust (see recipe below)
    pinch of salt

Ingredients for toasty oat crust:

 1 c. quick oats
 ½ c. pecans, chopped
 ⅓ c. brown sugar, packed
 ½ tsp. cinnamon
 ¾ c. butter, melted

Directions for toasty oat crust:

1. Preheat oven to 375 degrees F.
2. In medium bowl, combine all ingredients; mix well.
3. Press into bottom and sides of a very lightly oiled 9-inch pie plate.
4. Bake 8 to 10 minutes.

Directions for filling:

1. In top of double boiler, combine milk, sugar, and salt.
2. Cook over rapidly boiling water, stirring often until thickened (about 10 minutes).
3. Remove from heat and stir in half the nuts.
4. Pour into pie shell; sprinkle with remaining nuts.
5. Cool and top with whipped cream.

Black Bottom Pie

This is a rich, elegant-looking chocolate pie and a welcome treat for your Christmas dessert.

Ingredients:

1 chocolate cookie crumb crust (9-inch) (Use your favorite recipe or see recipe on page 219)
½ c. sugar
⅓ c. unsweetened cocoa
¼ c. butter
1 pkg. unflavored gelatin
¼ c. cold water
½ c. sugar
¼ c. cornstarch
2 c. milk
5 eggs, separated
1 tsp. vanilla extract
1 tsp. rum
½ c. sugar
   chocolate, grated

Directions:

1. In medium bowl, combine sugar, cocoa, and butter; set aside.
2. In small bowl, combine gelatin and cold water.
3. Place bowl in pan of simmering water to dissolve gelatin.
4. In medium saucepan, combine sugar, cornstarch, milk, and egg yolks.
5. Cook over medium heat, stirring constantly until mixture boils; boil and stir 1 minute.
6. Remove from heat; measure 1½ cup of the custard, and blend into cocoa-sugar mixture.
7. Add vanilla and pour into cooled crust; chill until set.
8. Combine dissolved gelatin with remaining custard.
9. Add rum; set aside.

10. In small bowl, beat egg whites until foamy, gradually add sugar, and beat until stiff peaks form.
11. Fold gelatin custard mixture into beaten egg whites.
12. Chill 15 minutes, or until partially set.
13. Spoon over chocolate custard in prepared crust.
14. Chill until set.
15. Garnish with grated chocolate before serving.

Cherry Pie

This is a beautiful presentation of an easy-to-make cherry pie for serving on Christmas Day.

Ingredients:

    1   unbaked pie shell (9-inch) (see page 219)
    1   can cherry pie filling
    12 oz. cream cheese, softened
    ½ c. sugar
    2   eggs
    ½ tsp. vanilla extract
    1   c. whipping cream, sweetened, as garnish

Directions:

1. Preheat oven to 425 degrees F.
2. Pour half of pie filling into prepared pie crust.
3. Bake 15 minutes.
4. Reduce oven to 350 degrees F.
5. In medium bowl, beat sugar, eggs, cream cheese, and vanilla until smooth.
6. Pour over baked pie filling.
7. Bake 25 minutes, or until done in the middle.
8. Cool completely.
9. Spoon remaining pie filling into the middle of the baked pie.
10. Spoon a dollop of sweetened whipped cream around the edge if desired and serve.

Chocolate Raspberry Cheesecake Pie

This chocolate raspberry cheesecake pie is wonderful.

Ingredients for cheesecake filling:

1   chocolate pie crust (recipe below)
2   pkg. cream cheese (3 oz. ea.), softened
1   can sweetened condensed milk (14 oz.)
1   egg
1   tsp. vanilla extract
1   can raspberries, drained

Ingredients for chocolate crust:

1½ c. chocolate cookie crumbs
1   Tbs. sugar
¼   c. butter, melted

Ingredients for chocolate glaze:

2   sq. semi-sweet baking chocolate (1 oz. ea.)
¼   c. whipping cream

Directions for cheesecake filling:

1. Preheat oven to 350 degrees F.
2. In large bowl, with electric mixer, beat cream cheese until fluffy.
3. Gradually beat in sweetened condensed milk until smooth.
4. Add egg and vanilla; mix well.
5. Arrange raspberries in bottom of chocolate crust.
6. Slowly pour cream cheese mixture over berries.
7. Bake 30 to 35 minutes, or until center is almost set.
8. Cool 1 hour.

Directions for chocolate crust:

1. In small bowl, combine cookie crumbs, sugar, and butter until thoroughly blended.

2. Press into 9-inch pie pan.

Direction for chocolate glaze:

1. In small saucepan, combine cream and chocolate.
2. Cook over low heat stirring constantly until chocolate melts and mixture thickens slightly.
3. Remove from heat.
4. Pour over cooled cheesecake; cool 30 minutes.
5. Refrigerate at least 2 hours.
6. Garnish with a few raspberries.
7. Store in refrigerator.

Yields: 1 pie.

Huckleberry Cheese Pie

Huckleberries are also great with cream cheese and sour cream. Try this excellent variation of huckleberry pie.

Ingredients:

2 pkg. cream cheese (8 oz. ea.)
½ c. sour cream
2 Tbs. sugar
1 c. huckleberry pie filling
1 graham cracker crust (see recipe on page 219)

Directions:

1. Preheat oven to 350 degrees F.
2. In medium bowl, blend cream cheese, sour cream, and sugar until smooth.
3. Pour into pie shell.
4. Top with huckleberry pie filling.
5. Sprinkle sugar on top.
6. Bake 5 minutes.
7. Remove from oven and cool on wire rack.
8. Chill before serving.

Chilled Raspberry Cream Pie

This is a refreshing and attractive chilled raspberry pie.

Ingredients:

1 baked pie shell (9-inch) (see page 218)
1 pkg. cream cheese (3 oz.)
½ c. powdered sugar
1 tsp. vanilla extract
½ pt. whipping cream
2 c. fresh raspberries
1 c. sugar
½ c. water
3 Tbs. cornstarch

Directions:

1. In small bowl, combine cream cheese, powdered sugar, and vanilla together; blend well.
2. Spread cream mixture onto bottom of pie shell.
3. In a saucepan, combine raspberries, sugar, water, and cornstarch.
4. Bring to boil, stirring constantly.
5. Cook until thickened.
6. Pour over cream mixture in pie shell.
7. Whip the cream and spread on top of cooled pie.
8. Top with fresh raspberries.

Cranberry Blueberry Pie

*This pie is a favorite with everyone. It is delicious warm with vanilla ice cream, or sweetened whipped cream.
Using a latticed pastry top will display the rich color of the luscious fruit filling.*

Ingredients:

2 c. fresh cranberries
2 c. blueberries, frozen, unsweetened
1½ c. sugar
⅓ c. flour

2   Tbs. butter
    pastry for 2-crust pie (see page 218)

Directions:

1. Preheat oven to 425 degrees F.
2. Put cranberries through food chopper.
3. In large bowl, combine cranberries, frozen blueberries, sugar, flour, and salt.
4. Place in pastry-lined 9-inch pie pan.
5. Dot with butter.
6. Adjust top crust, flute edges, and cut vents.
7. Bake 45 to 50 minutes, or until crust is golden.

Mince Pie

This is a delicious holiday pie for your family and friends.

Ingredients:

1 qt. homemade or commercially prepared mincemeat
½ c. sugar
1 tsp. salt
3 tsp. butter
½ c. molasses
    pastry for 2-crust pie (9-inch) (see page 218)

Directions:

1. Preheat oven to 350 degrees F.
2. Prepare pastry for a 9-inch, 2-crust pie.
3. In large bowl, combine mincemeat, sugar, salt, and molasses.
4. Adjust salt to taste if using commercially prepared mincemeat.
5. Pour ingredients pastry-lined pie pan.
6. Dot with butter.
7. Cover with the top crust.
8. Bake 30 minutes.

227

Irish Cream Chocolate Pie

This pie is a popular holiday favorite and very delicious. Your guests will enjoy this delightful treat.

Ingredients:

- 1 graham or chocolate crust (prepared or see page 219)
- 1 pkg. unflavored gelatin
- 1 tsp. vanilla extract
- ¾ c. milk
- ¾ c. Irish Cream
- ¾ c. chocolate chips, semi-sweet (6 oz.)
- 2 c. whipped cream, sweetened
  chocolate-dipped strawberries, for garnish

Directions:

1. In small saucepan, pour in milk. Sprinkle gelatin over milk; let stand 1 minute.
2. Stir over low heat until gelatin is dissolved, about 5 minutes.
3. Add chocolate and continue cooking, stirring constantly until chocolate is melted; stir in vanilla.
4. Remove from heat; stir occasionally, adding Irish Cream about 5 minutes after removal from heat.
5. When mixture forms mounds when dropped from spoon, fold in sweetened whipped cream.
6. Turn into crust.
7. Garnish with more whipped cream and strawberries if desired.
8. Chill at least 4 hours before serving.

Yields: 4 servings.

Did You Know? . . . .

Did you know that during Roman times, holly was a symbol of peace and good will?

Caramel Apple Pecan Pie

This recipe makes an interesting change from ordinary apple pie. The apples go well with caramel and pecans.

Ingredients:

    1 double pie shell, unbaked (see page 218)
    4 tart apples, peeled, cored, thinly sliced
    ¾ c. pecans, chopped
    ¼ c. sugar
    ¼ lb. caramels, coarsely chopped
    2 Tbs. flour
    ⅓ c. milk
       milk and sugar, for top

Directions:

1. Preheat oven to 375 degrees F.
2. Line the bottom of a 9-inch pie pan with half of pastry.
3. In large bowl, toss together apples, pecans, sugar, caramels, flour, and milk.
4. Spoon mixture into pie shell; top with remaining rolled out pastry.
5. Fold edge of top pastry under the bottom layer edge.
6. Pinch together and flute the edge.
7. Cut several slits in the top for steam to escape.
8. Brush top with milk and sprinkle with sugar.
9. Bake 45 minutes, or until crust is golden brown.
10. Cool to lukewarm on wire rack before slicing to serve.

Did You Know? . . . .

Did you know in England, people used to believe holly brought good luck and served as protection from witches?

Pumpkin Pie

*Our family loves pumpkin pie. It used to be my
daughter Brianne's favorite, and since she was vegetarian,
my husband made it often and also had her make it. She
had it so much that it is not her favorite, but now Caleb
asks us to make it frequently and Devontay likes it also.
We still consider this a family favorite, and the children eat
the leftovers for breakfast the next day.*

Ingredients:

    1½ c. sugar
    ½ tsp. salt
    2   tsp. ground cinnamon
    2   tsp. ground ginger
    1½ tsp. ground cloves
    4   eggs
    1   can pure pumpkin (29 oz.)
    2   cans evaporated milk (12 oz. ea.)
    2   unbaked deep-dish pie shells (9-inch)

Directions:

1. Preheat oven to 425 degrees F.
2. In small bowl, combine sugar, salt, cinnamon, ginger, and cloves.
3. In large bowl, beat eggs; stir in pumpkin and sugar-spice mixture.
4. Gradually stir in evaporated milk.
5. Pour into pie shells.
6. Bake 15 minutes; reduce heat to 350 degrees F.
7. Bake 40 to 45 minutes, or until inserted toothpick in center comes out clean.
8. Cool on wire rack 2 hours.
9. Serve immediately or refrigerate.
10. Serve warm with vanilla ice cream, or cold with sweetened vanilla flavored whipped cream.

Sweet Potato Pie

Sweet potatoes were another staple I grew up with. They were fairly inexpensive and were great baked or put in a pie.

Ingredients:

    4 lg. sweet potatoes
    2 c. sugar
    ½ c. butter
    1 pinch cinnamon
    1 pinch nutmeg
    ½ c. milk
    1 single pie crust or crushed vanilla wafers

Directions:

1. Preheat oven to 375 degrees F.
2. Boil sweet potatoes until tender. When pierced with fork, it should go in easy but not fall apart.
3. Let sweet potatoes cool and then peel them.
4. Put sweet potatoes in large mixing bowl and mash them thoroughly with a potato masher.
5. Melt the butter; pour it and the other ingredients into the bowl of potatoes; stir until well mixed.
6. Pour the sweet potato mixture into the crust.
7. Bake 35 to 40 minutes, or until inserted toothpick in center comes out clean.
8. Serve hot or cold.

Did You Know? . . . .

Did you know there are about 21,000 Christmas tree growers in the United States, and over 100,000 people employed full or part-time in the industry?

Dutch Apple Pie

This is a great recipe for those of you who love the Dutch version of the traditional apple pie. This pie is great with vanilla bean ice cream and dusted with cinnamon.

Ingredients for filling:

1   single-crust pastry (see page 218)
7   med. apples, peeled, cored, sliced
3½ Tbs. flour
1   c. sugar
¼   tsp. cloves
1   c. sour cream
1¾ tsp. cinnamon
1½ Tbs. sugar

Directions:

1. Preheat oven to 400 degrees F.
2. Fill pastry shell with sliced apples.
3. In medium bowl, combine flour, sugar, and cloves together.
4. Add sour cream, blend well, and pour over apples.
5. In small bowl, combine cinnamon with sugar; sprinkle over top.
6. Bake 10 minutes; reduce heat to 350 degrees F.
7. Continue baking for 40 to 50 minutes, or until filling becomes bubbly.
8. Place on wire rack to cool slightly.
9. Serve warm with vanilla ice cream or chill in refrigerator if desired.

Did You Know? . . . .

Did you know Christmas caroling began as an old English custom called Wassailing - toasting neighbors to a long and healthy life?

Christmas Delights Cookbook
A Collection of Christmas Recipes
Cookbook Delights Holiday Series Book 12

Preserving

Table of Contents

Page

A Basic Guide for Canning, Dehydrating, and Freezing

1. Place empty jars in hot, soapy water. Wash well inside and out with brush or soft cloth.
2. Run your finger around rim of each jar, discarding any that are chipped or cracked.
3. Rinse in clean, clear, very hot water, being careful to use tongs to avoid burning skin or fingers.
4. Place upside down on towel or fabric to drain well.
5. Place lids in boiling water bath for 2 minutes to sterilize and keep hot until ready to place on jar rims.
6. Immediately prior to filling jars with hot food, immerse in hot bath for 1 minute to heat jars. Heating jars avoids breakage.
7. If filling with room-temperature food, you need not immerse immediately prior to filling.
8. Fill jars with food to within ½ inch of neck of jars.
9. When ladling liquid over food, fill jars to 1 inch from top rim in each jar. This leaves air allowance for sealing purposes.
10. Wipe rims of jars with damp, clean cloth to remove any particles of food and again check for chips or cracks.
11. Using tongs, place lids from hot bath directly onto jars.
12. Place rings over lids, and using cloth, gloves, or holders, tighten down firmly while hanging onto jars.
13. Do not tighten down too hard as air may become trapped in jars and prevent them from sealing.
14. For fruits, tomatoes, and pickled vegetables, place each jar into water bath canning kettle so water covers jars by at least 1 inch.
15. For vegetables, process them in a pressure canner according to manufacturer's directions.
16. Follow time recommended for food being canned.
17. Do not mix jars of food in same canning kettle as times may vary for each kind of food.

18. At end of time recommended for canning, gently lift each jar out of bath with tongs, and place on protected surface.
19. Turn lids gently to be sure they are firmly tight.
20. Place filled, ringed jars on cloth to cool gradually.
21. Do not disturb rings, lids, or jars until sealed.
22. Lids will show slight indentation when sealed.
23. When cool, wipe jars with damp cloth then label and date each jar.
24. Leave overnight until thoroughly cooled.
25. Jars may then be stored upright on shelves.

Dehydrating

1. Always begin with fresh, good quality food that is clean and inspected for damage.
2. Pretreatment is not necessary, but food that is blanched will keep its color and flavor better. Use the same blanching times as you would for freezing. Fruit, especially, responds to pretreatment.
3. Doing some research on pretreatments may help you decide what procedure you would like to use.
4. You can marinate, salt, sweeten, or spice foods before you dehydrate them.
5. Jerky is meat that has been marinated and/or flavored by rubbing spices into it; avoid oil or grease of any kind as it will turn rancid as the food dries.
6. Vegetables and fruit can be treated the same way.
7. Slice or dice food thin and uniform so that it will dehydrate evenly. Uneven thicknesses may cause food to spoil because it did not dry as thoroughly as other parts.
8. Space food on dehydrator tray so that air can move around each piece.
9. Try not to let any piece touch another.
10. Fill your trays with all the same type of food as different foods take different amounts of time to dry.

11. You can, of course, dry different types of food at the same time, but you will have to remember to watch and remove the food that dehydrates more quickly. You can mix different foods in the same dehydrator batch, but do not mix strong vegetables like onions and garlic as other foods will absorb their taste while they are dehydrating.

12. The smaller the pieces, the faster a food will dehydrate. Thin leaves of spinach, celery, etc., will dry fastest. Remove them from the stalks before drying them or they will be overdone, losing flavor and quality. In very warm areas, they might even scorch. If they do, they will taste just like burned food when you rehydrate them.

13. Dense food like carrots will feel very hard when they are ready. Others will be crispy. Usually, a food that is high in fructose (sugar) will be leathery when it is finished dehydrating.

14. Remember that food smells when it is in the process of drying, so outdoors or in the garage is an excellent place to dry a big batch of those onions.

15. Always test each batch to make sure it is "done."

16. You can pasteurize finished food by putting it in a slow oven (150 degrees F.) for a few minutes.

17. Let the food cool before storing.

18. Store in airtight containers to guard against moisture. Jars saved from other food work well as long as they have lids that will keep moisture out.

19. Zip-closure food storage bags work well.

20. Jars of dehydrated carrots, celery, beets, etc., may look cheerful on your countertop, but the colors and flavors will fade. Dehydrated food keeps its color and flavor best if stored in a dark, cool place.

21. Dehydrating food takes time, so do not rush it. When you are all done, you will have a dried food stash to be proud of.

Freezing

1. Wash all containers and lids in hot, soapy water using soft cloth.
2. Rinse well in clear, clean, hot water.
3. Cool and drain well.
4. Place food into container to within 1 inch of rim. This allows for expansion of food during freezing.
5. Wipe rim of container with clean damp cloth, checking for chips or breaks.
6. Be certain cover fits the container snugly to avoid leaks. Burp air from container.
7. If food is hot when placing in container, cool prior to placing in freezer.
8. Label and date each container.
9. Store upright in freezer until frozen solid.

Canned Raspberries

It's always a good idea to stock up on raspberries when they are in season to enjoy year round.

Ingredients:

1 gal. fresh raspberries
4 c. water
3 c. sugar

Directions:

1. Rinse and drain raspberries.
2. Place in sterilized pint jars.
3. In a saucepan, bring water and sugar to boil over moderate high heat, stirring constantly.
4. Pour hot mixture over raspberries, leaving ⅜-inch space from the top.
5. Wipe rims, install sterilized lids, and adjust rings.
6. Process according to standard directions for canning found on page 234.

Yields: 8 pints.

Cherry Conserves

These conserves are delicious when served with toast and wonderful on pancakes or waffles.

Ingredients:

    5 lb. Bing cherries
    1 orange
    4 c. sugar (2 lb.)
    1 c. almonds or pecans, chopped
    1 c. seedless raisins
       juice of 1 lemon

Directions:

1. Wash and pit the cherries.
2. Wash, thinly slice, and seed the orange.
3. Put cherries and orange slices into a preserving kettle and add the lemon juice and sugar.
4. Cook the mixture uncovered about 45 minutes, stirring frequently until it is thick and transparent.
5. Remove from stove.
6. Skim off foam with metal spoon, add nuts and raisins, and cook another 10 minutes.
7. Ladle into hot, sterilized jars and seal immediately.

Apple Pie Filling

This makes a great pie filling to have on hand when you need to whip up a homemade pie and also doubles as a nice homemade gift for holiday gift giving.

Ingredients:

    60 apples, peeled, cored, and sliced
    4½ c. sugar
    ¼ tsp. nutmeg
    1   c. cornstarch
    1   tsp. salt

2 tsp. cinnamon
3 Tbs. lemon juice
1 c. water, cold
9 c. water

Directions:

1. Blend cornstarch in 1 cup of cold water.
2. Blend cornstarch mixture in a saucepan with all other ingredients, except the apples, and cook until thick and bubbly and sugar is dissolved.
3. Add 3 tablespoons lemon juice.
4. Fill quart jars tightly with sliced apples, cover with hot syrup.
5. Process according to standard directions for canning found on page 234.

Yields: 12 quarts.

Freezer Strawberry Jam

This is an easy-to-make strawberry jam and is always handy when frozen.

Ingredients:

2 c. strawberries, finely crushed
3 c. sugar
1 pkg. powdered fruit pectin
1 c. water

Directions:

1. Combine fruit and sugar.
2. Let stand 20 minutes, stirring occasionally.
3. Boil pectin and water rapidly for 1 minute, stirring constantly.
4. Remove from heat.
5. Add strawberries and stir about 2 minutes.
6. Follow standard directions for jams and jellies found on page 188.

7.   Cherry Preserves

These bright red cherry preserves are full of flavor and are wonderful served with homemade bread or biscuits right out of the oven with any pork dish.

Ingredients:

    1 qt. sour cherries
    4 c. sugar
    ½ c. light corn syrup

Directions:

1. Pit cherries.
2. Place cherries in saucepan with sugar and mix well.
3. Add corn syrup and bring all to a boil.
4. Cook 15 minutes, shaking pan occasionally.
5. Pour mixture into a shallow pan and allow to stand for 24 hours, stirring occasionally.
6. Ladle mixture into sterilized jars and follow standard directions for canning found on page 234.

Cherry and Raspberry Preserves

Cherries and raspberries make excellent fruit preserves.

Ingredients:

    2   lb. Bing cherries
    8   c. raspberries
    3½ c. sugar
    1   Tbs. fresh lemon juice

Directions:

1. Stem and pit the cherries.
2. In large bowl, stir together the cherries, raspberries, and sugar; let stand at room temperature, stirring occasionally, for 2 hours.
3. Pour the fruit into a wide, shallow, nonreactive saucepan, and stir in the lemon juice.

4. Cook over moderate heat, stirring occasionally, for 30 to 40 minutes until the mixture looks thickened and glazed.
5. Remove a spoonful of the preserves to a small saucer and chill in the freezer for 5 minutes.
6. Run your finger through the mixture; if it wrinkles it is ready to jar.
7. If it is not ready, continue cooking for 5 more minutes and repeat the test.
8. Ladle into jars and follow standard directions for canning on page 234.

Strawberry Margarita Preserves

This is a family favorite. It's great on English muffins and bagels.

Ingredients:

    6 c. strawberries, hulled and halved
    2 c. tart apples, peeled, cored, chopped
    ¼ c. lemon juice
    4 c. sugar
    ½ c. tequila
    7 tsp. triple sec
    2 tsp. strawberry schnapps

Directions:

1. In large stainless or enamel saucepan, combine berries, apples, and lemon juice.
2. Bring to a full rolling boil.
3. Add sugar, stirring constantly until sugar is dissolved.
4. Boil gently uncovered, about 40 minutes, stirring frequently until mixture reaches gel stage.
5. Remove from heat; stir in tequila and triple sec.
6. Return to heat; boil 5 minutes.
7. Ladle into clean, hot sterilized jars leaving ½-inch headspace.
8. Process 5 minutes at altitudes up to 1000 feet.

Yields: 6 half-pints.

Raspberry Preserves

You will have a hard time keeping these raspberry preserves in stock. They are marvelous.

Ingredients:

3 lb. raspberries to yield 4 c. crushed berries
6½ c. sugar
3 oz. liquid fruit pectin

Directions:

1. Wash jars in hot, soapy water and rinse. Place on a rack in the sink and pour boiling water in and over each jar. Drain.
2. Keep hot by transferring clean jars to a cookie tray and placing in a 200 degree F. oven.
3. Prepare lids by placing in a saucepan of gently boiling water.
4. Prepare raspberries by removing stems and caps.
5. Place in a sink of cold water and stir gently with your hands for 5 seconds.
6. Lift the raspberries into a colander to drain.
7. Place raspberries in food processor and process 15 seconds until puréed.
8. Measure raspberries into a 6 or 8-quart pot.
9. Stir the sugar into the berries and mix well.
10. Bring to full rolling boil over high heat, stirring constantly.
11. Add fruit pectin and return to full rolling boil.
12. Boil hard for 1 minute, stirring constantly to prevent scorching.
13. If you prefer fewer seeds in the jam, you can skim off some that float to the top with the foam.
14. Remove from heat, skim, and discard any foam using a metal spoon.
15. Ladle jam into a liquid measuring cup and fill the jars immediately to within ⅛-inch of the top.
16. Wipe jar rims and threads with a clean, damp cloth.

17. Remove jar lids from boiling water using tongs and place on a paper towel. Wipe dry.
18. Place lids on the jars and screw on tightly.
19. Place jars on sturdy rack in a canner or large saucepan of boiling water to cover the jars by 1 to 2 inches.
20. Place the lid on the canner and bring water back to a boil. Boil 10 minutes for 8-ounce jars.
21. Remove jars from the canner and let cool.
22. Check the seals after 1 hour to make sure the lids are curving down.
23. Warning: Jars and lids are very hot. Use clean, damp dishcloths or wear padded gloves to screw the lids on the jam-filled jars.
24. Raspberry preserves are delicious used as a cake filling, in tarts, spooned over plain yogurt, ice cream, or pancakes.

Yields: 7 jars (8 oz.).

Drying Cranberries

1. Use dried cranberries the same as you use raisins.
2. Put them in hot and cold cereals, in salads, and in trail mixes.
3. To start, wash cranberries, and plunge them into boiling water for 15 to 30 seconds, just until the skin pops.
4. Immediately stop the cooking action by placing berries in ice water.
5. Drain on paper towels.
6. Preheat oven to 350 degrees F.
7. Place cranberries on baking sheet.
8. Place in oven.
9. Turn oven off, and let cranberries sit overnight or until sticky and no longer wet.
10. Once dry, keep them in the refrigerator or the freezer.

Raspberry Fruit Leather

This raspberry fruit leather is a favorite way of preserving. It is so easy to take on trips, put in lunches, and we enjoy these any time for snacks.

Ingredients:

    4 c. raspberry purée
    ¼ c. honey for sweetening, or use your own preference

Directions:

1. Purée fruit in blender.
2. For sweetening, add 1 tablespoon honey for every 1 cup of purée if desired. Or use corn syrup which prevents the formation of crystals and is best for long storage. May also substitute sugar, lemon, or orange juice. May use saccharin-based sweetener. Some prefer no sweetening at all, so use your own taste preference.
3. If using oven, line baking sheet with freezer wrap, extending it over the edges. A very light spray of nonstick cooking oil is recommended.
4. Spread purée ¼-inch thick around the edges, ⅛-inch thick in the center.
5. Dry in the sun, or the oven at 140 degrees F., or in a dehydrator at 135 degrees F. following the manufacturer's directions.
6. Ready when sheet is leathery and not sticky to the touch, usually 4 to 10 hours.
7. Pull from freezer paper while still warm, and roll in plastic wrap, jellyroll fashion. If desired, use scissors to cut the roll into serving pieces.
8. Cool; pack in airtight containers.
9. Can be stored in dark place for 30 days at room temperature, months in the refrigerator; years in the freezer.

10. Raspberry fruit leather is great alone or in combination with cranberries, strawberries, blueberries, peaches, or apples. You may be even more daring and blend three fruits.
11. Orange juice is a nice liquid addition (which may be necessary if using fresh fruit; it's unlikely you'll need it with thawed frozen raspberries).
12. For extra zing, try adding a touch of cinnamon.

Cherry Dill Pickles

The cherry leaves add flavor and presentation to these pickles.

Ingredients:

5   qt. cucumbers
5   qt. water
1   c. pickling salt
15 c. sugar
10 c. vinegar
     lg. bunch cherry leaves
     lg. bunch fresh dill
     pickling spices

Directions:

1. Layer cucumbers, dill, and cherry leaves in crock.
2. Mix 5 quarts of water to 1 cup salt for brine.
3. Pour over cucumbers; soak for 10 days.
4. After the 10 days, wash pickles and put into clean jars with ½ teaspoon pickling spices per jar.
5. In large pot, combine sugar and vinegar; bring to boil.
6. Pour boiling hot syrup over pickles.
7. Clean jar edge and seal tightly.

Yields: 12 quarts.

Vegetable Juice Cocktail

Try this delicious and healthy juice for your own use, and to give as gifts.

Ingredients:

15 lb. fresh tomatoes
2 c. celery, chopped
3 lg. onions, peeled, cut into chunks
1 green bell pepper, seeded, chopped
2 med. beets
4 carrots
3 garlic cloves, peeled
¼ c. sugar
1 tsp. black pepper
2 tsp. prepared horseradish
⅓ c. lemon juice
6 qt. water, or as needed
1 Tbs. hot sauce, or to taste
1 c. sugar
¼ c. salt, or to taste

Directions:

1. Use a juicer to process the tomatoes, celery, onion, green pepper, beets, carrots, and garlic.
2. Place all of the juice into a large pot.
3. Stir in sugar, black pepper, horseradish, lemon juice, and enough water to make a thin consistency.
4. Season with hot sauce, to taste.
5. Bring to boil; continue boiling for 20 minutes.
6. Ladle into 1-quart jars leaving ¾-inch headspace.
7. Stir 1 tablespoon sugar and 1 teaspoon salt into each jar.
8. Wipe rims clean; place lids and rings onto jars.
9. Process in a pressure canner for 35 minutes at 10 pounds of pressure.

Christmas Delights Cookbook
A Collection of Christmas Recipes
Cookbook Delights Holiday Series Book 12

Salads

Table of Contents

Page

Almond Turkey Salad

Try this colorful turkey salad with your leftover holiday turkey.

Ingredients:

½ c. mayonnaise
2 Tbs. sour cream
1 tsp. sugar
¼ c. cider vinegar
1 tsp. salt
1 c. turkey, chopped
4 eggs, hard-boiled, diced
½ c. almonds, blanched, quartered
1 c. celery, finely chopped
1 Tbs. pickle relish
8 black olives, sliced
½ red bell pepper, cut into thin strips
¼ c. green onions, including tops, sliced
1 jalapeno pepper, stemmed, seeded, finely chopped

Directions:

1. In small bowl, combine mayonnaise, sour cream, sugar, vinegar, and salt to make dressing.
2. In medium bowl, combine turkey, eggs, almonds, celery, pickle relish, olives, red pepper, green onions, and jalapeno pepper.
3. Add dressing to turkey mixture and mix thoroughly.
4. Chill.
5. Serve in cups of lettuce, and garnish with tomato wedges.
6. If you prefer, you can serve salad on tomato slices that have been arranged on individual beds of lettuce.

Yields: 6 servings.

Angel Salad with Peach Halo

The taste of this salad is interesting, and it's very good.

Ingredients:

- 1 can cling peaches, sliced, drained, reserve syrup
- 1 Tbs. unflavored gelatin
- 3 Tbs. lemon juice
- 2 pkg. cream cheese (3 oz. ea.)
- ½ c. mayonnaise
- ¼ tsp. salt
- 1 tsp. prepared horseradish
- ½ c. walnuts, chopped
- ½ c. evaporated milk, chilled
- ¾ c. celery, finely chopped
  - cherries and peaches, for garnish
  - sweetened whipped cream

Directions:

1. Drain peaches.
2. Heat ¾ cup syrup from drained peaches to boiling.
3. In small bowl, soften gelatin in lemon juice and dissolve in hot syrup.
4. Allow to cool.
5. Mash cheese with fork.
6. Blend in mayonnaise and seasonings.
7. Blend in gelatin mixture.
8. In chilled bowl, whip chilled evaporated milk in until fluffy.
9. Fold in gelatin mixture, celery, walnuts, and peach slices, withholding 7 peach slices for garnish.
10. Turn into 8-inch ring mold.
11. Chill until firm.
12. Unmold on greens.
13. Decorate with peaches and cherries, and top with sweetened whipped cream.

Apple Cabbage Salad

Try this apple cabbage combination. It makes for an extra delicious and healthy salad.

Ingredients for salad:

> 6 c. cabbage, shredded
> 2 delicious apples (1 red, 1 gold), cored, chopped

Ingredients for dressing:

> ¼ c. sugar
> 3 tsp. cider vinegar
> 1 tsp. cornstarch
> 2 Tbs. mayonnaise
> ½ tsp. celery seed
> 3 Tbs. plain yogurt
> ¼ tsp. salt
> ⅛ tsp. dry mustard
> ¾ c. water

Directions:

1. In 2-cup microwave-safe cup or bowl, combine sugar, cornstarch, celery seed, salt, and dry mustard.
2. Gradually stir in water and vinegar until smooth.
3. Microwave, uncovered, on high 3 minutes, or until mixture boils and thickens slightly, stirring once.
4. Refrigerate 3 hours, or until chilled.
5. Blend together with mayonnaise and yogurt.
6. Combine cabbage and apples in serving bowl.
7. Pour chilled dressing over cabbage mixture.
8. Toss lightly to coat.

Did You Know? . . . .

Did you know we kiss under the mistletoe because the ancient Norse associated mistletoe with their goddess of love?

Candied Pecan Greens

This is a nice salad for your holiday lunch or dinner with baby greens dotted with festive cranberries and pecans.

Ingredients for salad:

6   c. baby greens
2   Tbs. sugar
¼   c. pecans, chopped
⅛   c. red onion, finely chopped
¼   c. dried cranberries

Ingredients for dressing:

¼   c. olive oil
1½ Tbs. sugar
2   Tbs. balsamic vinegar
¼   tsp. salt
1   pinch black pepper

Directions:

1. Wash salad greens and place in large bowl.
2. Whisk dressing ingredients together.
3. In small skillet, over medium heat, caramelize sugar and pecans until golden.
4. Pour into small oiled pan and cool.
5. Break apart into bite-size pieces.
6. Just before serving, toss lettuce with the pecans, onions, and cranberries.
7. Toss again with the dressing.

Did You Know? . . . .

Did you know the growth of mistletoe is parasitic on trees?

Lettuce with Berry Vinaigrette

The raspberry vinegar adds great flavor to this light salad, and it is a great dish to begin your holiday meal. Try this delightful salad.

Ingredients:

    4 c. baby lettuce leaves
    4 Tbs. raspberry vinegar
    2 Tbs. olive oil
    2 Tbs. rich vegetable stock
    1 tsp. oregano, chopped
    1 tsp. chives, chopped
       dash of black pepper

Directions:

1. In small bowl, stir together oil, vinegar, and vegetable stock in.
2. Add herbs as close to serving time as possible.
3. Toss dressing with baby lettuce and serve.

Barley and Veggie Salad

This is a unique salad using barley which is delicious, and a nice complementary dish with your holiday meal.

Ingredients:

    2 c. pearl barley, cooked, cooled, divided
    3 c. water
    1 c. celery, chopped
    ½ c. green onions, chopped
    ½ c. zucchini, chopped
    ½ c. black olives, chopped
    ½ c. canned artichoke hearts, chopped
    ½ c. fresh tomato, diced
    2 oz. feta cheese, crumbled
       Italian dressing

Directions:

1. Boil ¾ cup uncooked barley in water for 40 minutes until tender; cool.
2. In medium bowl, combine remaining ingredients, adding enough Italian dressing to coat well. Chill.
3. Serve on lettuce leaves or use to fill fresh tomato.

Yields: 4 to 6 servings.

Berries and Cherries Rosé

This makes a tasty, colorful holiday salad.

Ingredients:

1 Tbs. unflavored gelatin
2 Tbs. sugar
¾ c. water, boiling
1½ c. rosé wine
½ c. raspberries and halved strawberries
1 c. sweet cherries, pitted

Directions:

1. In medium bowl, mix gelatin and sugar.
2. Add boiling water, and stir until gelatin dissolves completely.
3. Stir in wine.
4. Refrigerate, stirring occasionally, until mixture begins to thicken and becomes syrupy.
5. Fold in berries and cherries.
6. Pour into a 4-cup mold or six ¾-cup molds.
7. Refrigerate 3 to 4 hours, or until firm.
8. Serve with whipped cream.

Yields: 6 servings.

Gorgonzola Salad

I usually make a double amount of dressing and store it in my refrigerator in a glass jar. I also buy my Gorgonzola cheese in a big chunk and store it in my freezer.

Ingredients:

1 tsp. salt
1 tsp. red wine vinegar
½ c. olive oil, extra light
3 garlic cloves, crushed
1 head lettuce
1 oz. Gorgonzola cheese, crumbled

Directions:

1. In small bowl, whisk salt, vinegar, olive oil, and garlic together; set aside.
2. Chop lettuce and arrange in salad bowls.
3. Sprinkle some Gorgonzola cheese over each salad.
4. Spoon on desired amount of dressing, and serve.

Yields: 10 servings.

Blue Heaven with Raspberry

This is a festive combination of blue cheese and raspberries.

Ingredients for salad:

1 head lettuce, butter or Boston bib
½ c. blue cheese, crumbled
½ c. pecan halves, fried lightly in olive oil
½ c. raspberries

Ingredients for dressing:

½ c. raspberries, whole fresh or frozen
½ c. raspberry vinegar
½ c. honey
1 c. olive oil

Directions for salad:

1. Wash, drain, and break apart the lettuce.
2. Be sure to use the tiny leaves in the middle.
3. Top with remaining ingredients and serve with raspberry dressing.

Directions for dressing:

1. In food processor or blender, place raspberries, vinegar, and honey.
2. Turn on processor or blender; slowly add olive oil.

Zippy Cabbage Salad

This cabbage salad has enough bite to make it a favorite.

Ingredients:

½ head green cabbage
2 tomatoes, diced
2 avocados, diced
4 fresh jalapeno, thin slices, diced
2 sprigs cilantro, chopped
½ lemon, juiced
   salt and pepper, to taste

Directions:

1. Slice cabbage like coleslaw.
2. Chop tomato, avocado, jalapeño, and cilantro.
3. Place all in large bowl; squirt lemon juice on mixture.
4. Add salt and pepper, to taste, mix thoroughly.
5. Serve immediately.

Broccoli Onion Salad

I love bacon, and combined with red onion and raisins, this broccoli salad is absolutely delicious.

Ingredients:

    4 c. broccoli, chopped into bite-size pieces, to taste
    ½ c. red onion, chopped
    ⅓ c. raisins
    ⅓ c. sunflower seeds
    1 c. mayonnaise
    2 Tbs. sugar
    2 Tbs. lemon juice
    8 slices bacon, cooked, crumbled
       salt and pepper, to taste

Directions:

1. In large bowl, combine broccoli, onions, raisins, and sunflower seeds; set aside.
2. Combine mayonnaise, sugar, lemon juice, salt and pepper, to taste.
3. Fold dressing into salad mixture.
4. Refrigerate.
5. Add bacon just before serving.

Cranapple and Fennel Salad

This salad is a very "woodsy" combination of apples, fennel, and cranberries. Try this blend of flavors for an unusual treat.

Ingredients:

    1½ fennel bulb
    1½ red delicious apple, thinly sliced, unpeeled
    ½ c. pecans, toasted, chopped
    3 Tbs. lemon juice
    3 Tbs. olive oil
    ⅛ tsp. salt
    ¼ tsp. pepper

½ c. Parmesan cheese, freshly grated
dried cranberries, finely chopped
fresh fennel fronds, for garnish (optional)

Directions:

1. Trim base from fennel bulb; cut bulb in half, and thinly slice, reserving fennel fronds for garnish if desired.
2. In medium bowl, stir fennel, apple, pecans, lemon juice, oil, and seasonings together.
3. Stir in cheese and cranberries.
4. Cover, refrigerate, and chill until ready to serve.
5. Garnish with fennel fronds for appearance and taste, if desired.

Festive Holiday Salad

This is a refreshing salad you will enjoy during the holidays.

Ingredients:

1 lb. baby greens, rinsed
2 lb. oranges
2 lb. pomegranate
3 lb. dried cranberries
1 c. frozen raspberries, thawed
¾ c. lime juice, freshly squeezed
⅓ c. raspberry vinegar
4 Tbs. honey
salt and pepper, to taste

Directions:

1. Wash and dry greens.
2. In large bowl, gently toss together oranges, pomegranates, and cranberries.
3. In blender, combine raspberries, lime juice, vinegar, honey, salt and pepper, to taste; blend until creamy.
4. To serve, plate the greens, top with fruit mix, and drizzle vinaigrette lightly over salad.
5. Adjust the seasonings.

Christmas Turkey Taco Salad

This is a delicious way to use your leftover turkey.

Ingredients:

3 flour tortillas
½ lb. ground turkey
⅓ c. water
1 tsp. chili power
¼ tsp. garlic powder
¼ tsp. cayenne pepper
1 can kidney beans, drained (8 oz.)
5 c. lettuce, shredded
1 tomato, chopped
½ c. Monterey jack cheese, shredded
¼ c. onion, chopped
¼ c. Thousand Island dressing
¼ c. sour cream
4 ripe olives, pitted, sliced

Directions:

1. Preheat oven to 400 degrees F.
2. Cut tortillas into 12 wedges or 3 x ¼-inch strips and place in 15½ x 10½ x 1-inch ungreased jellyroll pan.
3. Bake 6 to 8 minutes, stirring at least once, until golden brown and crisp. Cool.
4. Grind leftover turkey and place in medium pan.
5. Stir in water, chili powder, salt, garlic powder, red pepper, and kidney beans.
6. Heat to boiling, reduce heat, and simmer, uncovered, 2 to 3 minutes, stirring occasionally until liquid is absorbed.
7. Cool 10 minutes.
8. In large bowl, mix lettuce, tomato, cheese, and onion together.

9. Toss with dressing, and divide between 4 dinner plates.
10. Top each salad with about ½ cup turkey mixture.
11. Arrange tortilla wedges around salad, and garnish with sour cream and olives.

Cole Slaw

Traditional cole slaw is always great with a meal.

Ingredients:

5   lb. cabbage, shredded (about 20 c.)
5   c. carrots, shredded
1½ c. green pepper, chopped
1   c. onion, chopped
¼   c. water, cold
1   pkg. unflavored gelatin
1⅔ c. sugar
1⅔ c. cider vinegar
1½ Tbs. salt
¼   tsp. pepper
1   Tbs. celery seed (optional)
1⅔ c. canola oil

Directions:

1. In large bowl, combine prepared cabbage, carrot, green pepper, and onion.
2. Cover and refrigerate until well chilled.
3. In small cup, soften gelatin in cold water.
4. In medium saucepan, measure sugar, vinegar, salt, pepper, and celery seed; bring to boil.
5. Remove from heat, add softened gelatin.
6. Cool slightly to thicken; beat in oil gradually.
7. Toss vegetables with dressing.
8. Keep refrigerated.
9. Before serving, toss salad once more.

Cranberry Orange Salad

This gelatin salad can be made low calorie by substituting sugar free gelatin for regular gelatin, and is delicious either way.

Ingredients:

1 med. orange
1 pkg. red gelatin
½ c. raw cranberries
¾ c. water, boiling
½ c. water, cold
1 Tbs. sugar
   ice cubes

Directions:

1. Quarter the orange and remove seeds.
2. In food processor or blender, combine orange and cranberries and chop finely.
3. Add sugar; process to mix; set aside.
4. Dissolve gelatin in boiling water.
5. In large bowl, combine cold water and enough ice cubes to make 1 cup ice water.
6. Add water to gelatin and stir.
7. Set aside until ice cubes melt.
8. Add fruit mixture.
9. Pour into a 2-cup mold or an 8-inch square pan which has been sprayed with nonstick coating.
10. Chill until firm.

Did You Know? . . . .

Did you know mistletoe in the Middle Ages was considered mysterious and even sacred?

Christmas Delights Cookbook
A Collection of Christmas Recipes
Cookbook Delights Holiday Series Book 12

Side Dishes

Table of Contents

Page

Apple Walnut Sage Stuffing

The combination of apples and walnuts add great flavor and texture to this recipe.

Ingredients:

¼ lb. bacon, chopped
½ c. butter
¾ c. onion, finely diced
¾ c. carrot, finely diced
¾ c. celery, finely diced
4 lg. apples, unpeeled, finely diced
1 tsp. thyme
2 bay leaves
1 c. fresh sage, chopped
2 Tbs. fresh parsley, chopped
1 tsp. cinnamon
1 c. apple juice
1 c. chicken stock
8 c. coarse bread crumbs
1 c. walnuts, crushed
    salt and pepper, to taste

Directions:

1. In large skillet, cook bacon until almost crisp.
2. Add butter; sauté onion, carrot, and celery for 6 to 8 minutes.
3. Add apples, thyme, bay leaves, sage, parsley, and cinnamon.
4. Cook for another 5 minutes, and then add apple juice and chicken stock.
5. Bring to boil; remove from heat.
6. Place mixture in a large mixing bowl to cool.
7. Add walnuts and bread crumbs.
8. Mix well and season with salt and pepper.

9. Use to stuff your choice of meat, or place in a covered, buttered baking dish and bake in a preheated oven at 350 degrees F. for about 30 minutes.

Turkey Gravy

This is a simple and basic turkey gravy that tastes great every time.

Ingredients:

3 c. water
½ c. water, cool
2 cans turkey or chicken broth
½ c. flour
turkey giblets
salt and pepper, to taste

Directions:

1. Rinse giblets under cold water, place in a saucepan with 3 cups water, and bring to a boil.
2. Cover and reduce heat to a mild simmer for 1 hour.
3. Turn off heat, leave covered, and set aside.
4. Remove roasted turkey from roasting pan.
5. Skim off fat, and place the roasting pan on 2 burners turned to medium-high heat.
6. Add broth from the simmered giblets to the roasting pan, 2 cans turkey or chicken broth, and if available, the water from boiled potatoes (if serving with your dinner).
7. In small cup, mix flour with ½ cup water and blend with a fork or whisk.
8. Pour flour mixture slowly into boiling liquid in roasting pan, stirring and cooking until bubbling and thickened, about 10 minutes.
9. Season to taste with salt and pepper.

Cranberry-Apricot Sauce

This cranberry sauce is unique with the addition of apricots and ginger. It is also full of vitamins.

Ingredients:

    14 apricots, dried, each cut into 3 strips
    ½ c. cranberry juice
    12 oz. cranberries, fresh or frozen, thawed
    ½ c. sugar plus 1 Tbs.
    1 Tbs. ginger, fresh, pared, minced

Directions

1. In medium saucepan, soak dried apricots in cranberry juice for 10 minutes.
2. Add remaining ingredients and stir well.
3. Cook over medium heat for about 5 minutes, stirring occasionally until the cranberries have popped and the syrup has thickened slightly.
4. Let the sauce cool to room temperature, then cover and refrigerate it until its cold.
5. The sauce can be stored in the refrigerator for up to 1 week.
6. Transfer sauce to serving dish and serve cold.
7. The colder the better, as long as it isn't frozen.

Yields: 6 servings.

Wild Rice Stuffing

My husband and I enjoy wild rice, and this makes a great stuffing.

Ingredients:

    3½ c. chicken stock
    2 c. wild rice
    1 lb. sausage (chicken or turkey)
    3 Tbs. butter
    2 garlic cloves, minced
    ½ white onion, finely diced
    3 celery stalks, finely diced

⅓ c. parsley, finely chopped
⅓ c. almonds, slivered
⅔ c. Parmesan cheese, grated
    salt and pepper, to taste

Directions:

1. In large saucepan, bring chicken stock to boil.
2. Stir in rice; reduce heat, cover, and cook 25 minutes until done.
3. In a skillet, cook sausage until brown.
4. Drain grease; add butter, garlic, onion, and celery.
5. Cook 2 minutes.
6. Remove from heat and toss with add-ins and rice.

Baked Squash Dish

This makes a flavorful squash dish. Enjoy.

Ingredients:

2 lb. yellow squash, cooked, drained well
1 sm. onion, diced
2 Tbs. butter
3 lg. eggs
½ tsp. salt
¼ c. light brown sugar
½ c. saltines, crushed
1 c. half and half cream (8 oz.)
¼ tsp. vanilla extract

Directions:

1. Preheat oven to 375 degrees F.
2. Lightly grease a baking dish.
3. Place cooked squash in large bowl.
4. In small skillet, sauté onion in butter.
5. Add eggs to squash and blend well.
6. Add onions and butter to squash and blend.
7. Add salt and brown sugar.
8. Add cracker crumbs alternately with half and half.
9. Add vanilla; mix well.
10. Pour into greased baking dish.
11. Bake 45 minutes.

Cornbread Stuffing

Our family likes this cornbread stuffing. This is a tasty change from the usual bread stuffing.

Ingredients:

½ c. butter
2 c. onion, chopped
1 c. celery, chopped
2 c. chicken broth, or vegetable broth for vegetarians
1 can whole kernel corn
2 cans green chilies, diced
3 Tbs. parsley
½ tsp. paprika
½ tsp. salt
⅛ tsp. black pepper
¼ tsp. dried oregano
6 c. cornbread
1 c. pecans, chopped

Directions:

1. Preheat oven to 350 degrees F.
2. Grease a 2½-quart baking dish with butter, set aside.
3. In large skillet, over low heat, melt butter.
4. Cook onion and celery until tender, 5 to 8 minutes.
5. Stir in chicken broth, corn, green chilies, parsley, paprika, salt, pepper, and oregano.
6. Mix well.
7. Add cornbread and pecans; mix to incorporate.
8. Spoon into prepared baking dish.
9. Bake 45 minutes to 1 hour, or until golden brown.
10. When stuffing a roasting hen, turkey, or roast, make sure the meat is well done.

Cranberry Chutney

We have been introduced to chutneys with the arrival of our daughter from India.

Ingredients:

1¾ lb. tart apples, chopped
2¼ lb. cranberries
2   c. light brown sugar
1¼ c. cider vinegar
½   Tbs. cinnamon
½   Tbs. salt
½   Tbs. ground ginger
¾   tsp. ground cloves
¾   tsp. pepper flakes
½   lb. dark raisins

Directions:

1. Place all ingredients in saucepan, and cook 25 to 30 minutes.
2. Remove from heat and let cool.
3. Refrigerate.

Yield: 8 servings.

Did You Know? . . . .

Did you know that in Spain children leave their shoes under the Christmas tree the night of January 5th and presents from the Three Kings (Los Reyes Magos: Melchor, Gaspar, and Baltasar) appear the next morning? Santa Claus is called Papa Noel and some children receive presents both days: on December 24th (from Papa Noel) and on January 6th (from the Three Kings).

Kartoshnik, Cheese, and Onions

This looks like a cake when baked but is eaten like a potato.

Ingredients:

3 lg. potatoes, peeled, quartered
5 eggs
¼ c. heavy whipping cream
¾ tsp. salt
¾ c. Cheddar cheese, sharp, shredded
¾ c. Swiss cheese, shredded
½ onion, chopped
3 tsp. baking powder
½ c. butter, melted
½ c. sour cream
½ c. green onions, chopped

Directions:

1. In medium saucepan, cover potatoes with water and boil until cooked.
2. When done, drain water and discard.
3. Mash potatoes and set aside.
4. Preheat oven to 450 degrees F.
5. Prepare a 9 x 9-inch ovenproof baking dish by spraying with nonstick canola spray or rub inside with butter.
6. In separate bowl, beat eggs and add whipping cream and salt.
7. Whisk until blended.
8. Add mashed potatoes; mix until well blended.
9. Add both cheeses and onions and stir well.
10. Add baking powder and mix well.
11. Pour potato mixture into prepared baking dish and level.

12. Bake 35 minutes, or until top is a nice light-brown color.
13. Remove from oven and let cool for 5 minutes.
14. The Kartoshnik will rise when cooking, but will settle when removed from oven and cooled slightly.
15. In small saucepan, melt butter.
16. Cut Kartoshnik into 3 x 3-inch squares and serve with melted butter, a dollop of sour cream, and a sprinkling of green onions.
17. You can also use plain yogurt, or low fat sour cream.

Yields: 11 servings.

Cranberry Mead Applesauce

Cranberries and mead add great flavor to this applesauce.

Ingredients:

4 Granny Smith apples
¾ c. whole cranberries
½ c. bun ratty mead
¼ c. water
½ c. sugar

Directions:

1. Wash, core, and quarter apples.
2. Combine with cranberries in saucepan.
3. Add mead and water; cover.
4. Cook over low heat until apples are mushy, stirring often to prevent sticking.
5. Add sugar and cook further until sugar is absorbed.
6. Remove from heat; cool 30 minutes.
7. Blend in processor for 10 seconds.

Oyster Stuffing

This is enough for a 14 to 15-pound turkey. If you like oysters, you will love this oyster dressing.

Ingredients:

1	lb. bread, including crusts (10 c. packed, cubed)
1	pt. oysters, raw
4-8	Tbs. butter
1	c. celery, finely chopped
2	c. onions, chopped
¼-½	c. fresh parsley, minced
1	Tbs. sage, minced
1	Tbs. thyme, minced
¾	tsp. salt
½	tsp. black pepper, ground
¼	tsp. nutmeg, freshly grated
⅛	tsp. cloves, ground
1	c. chicken stock
2	lg. eggs, well beaten (optional)

Directions:

1. Preheat oven to 400 degrees F., toast bread on middle rack, and turn into large bowl.
2. Melt butter in skillet; add onions, celery, and cook 5 minutes until tender.
3. Remove from heat and stir in the spices.
4. Stir in bread cubes and drained oysters; toss until the stuffing is moist, but not packed together.
5. Stir in stock and eggs and put in bird while moist.
6. Note: If cooked in a casserole dish, use oyster juice in place of some of the stock and cook at 350 degrees F. for 25 to 40 minutes.

Yields: 8 servings.

Cheddar Mashed Potatoes

These are delicious potatoes and make a very hearty side dish. They are just as delicious without bacon, for any vegetarians in your household.

Ingredients:

    3   lb. russet potatoes, peeled, cut in 1-inch cubes
    5   garlic cloves, quartered
    1   c. buttermilk, warm
    1¼ c. Cheddar cheese, shredded
    4   Tbs. fresh chives, chopped
    10 slices bacon (leave out for vegetarian)
        salt and pepper, to taste

Directions:

1. In large, heavy saucepan, place potatoes and garlic; add enough cold water to cover.
2. Over high heat, bring to boil.
3. Reduce heat to medium-high, cover, and cook for 15 to 20 minutes, or until the potatoes are fork tender; drain well.
4. In skillet, cook bacon, crumble, and set aside.
5. Return potatoes to saucepan; toss to evaporate any water.
6. Coarsely mash the potatoes with the buttermilk, making sure to leave the majority of potatoes in large chunks.
7. Gently mix in remaining ingredients.
8. Serve hot.

Yields: 12 servings.

Did You Know? . . . .

Did you know that in England, Christmas is rung in starting on December 21ˢᵗ?

Cheesy Scalloped Potatoes

It is always good to have a quick potato dish to add as a side dish. We prefer the taste of red potatoes.

Ingredients:

    2 lb. red potatoes
    1 yellow onion, thinly sliced (optional)
    2 c. Cheddar cheese, shredded
    2 c. cream
    ½ tsp. salt
    ½ tsp fresh ground pepper

Directions:

1. Preheat oven to 425 degrees F.
2. Lightly grease a 9 x 13-inch baking pan.
3. Peel potatoes and slice very thin.
4. In large bowl, combine potato slices with onion.
5. Add cheese, cream, salt, and pepper; mix well.
6. Pour into prepared baking pan.
7. Cover with foil; bake 40 minutes.
8. Uncover; bake 5 to 10 minutes until golden.

Squash Fritters

These make a unique dish that is very flavorful.

Ingredients:

    ½ c. milk
    1   egg, lightly beaten
    1   c. flour
    1½ tsp. baking powder
    ½ oz. ranch dip mix
    2   c. shredded squash
        canola oil, for frying

Directions:

1. Fill deep-fat fryer or deep skillet with canola oil to a 2-inch depth. Heat oil to 375 degrees F.
2. In mixing bowl, combine milk and egg.
3. In small bowl, stir together dry ingredients and add to egg mixture; blend well.
4. Fold in squash.
5. Drop batter by rounded teaspoonfuls into hot oil.
6. Fry until deep golden brown, turning once.
7. Drain thoroughly on paper towels.

Hot Fruit Casserole

This is a unique fruit side dish.

Ingredients:

1 can pineapple, sliced (1 lb.), drained
1 can apricot halves (1 lb.), drained
1 can peach halves in syrup (1 lb.), drained
1 lb. strawberries, fresh or frozen, halved
⅓ c. butter
2 tsp. curry powder
1 c. brown sugar
2 Tbs. cornstarch

Directions:

1. Preheat oven to 350 degrees F.
2. Lightly butter a casserole dish.
3. In large bowl, combine all the fresh and drained fruits and pour into prepared dish.
4. In small saucepan, melt butter and curry powder together until bubbly; then add brown sugar and corn starch.
5. Drizzle this evenly over the fruit; cover with foil.
6. Bake 45 minutes.

Yields: 4 servings.

Steamed Artichokes in Butter

The traditional way to eat steamed artichokes is to pull one artichoke leaf out at a time and scrape the tender meat from the bottom of the leaf with your teeth. Be sure to remove the thistle-like choke in the center of the artichoke before enjoying the meaty heart. We prefer the melted butter versions for warm artichokes and the vinaigrette sauces for serving chilled.

Ingredients:

> 4 lg. globe artichokes
> 1 lemon, halved
> 1 tsp. sea salt

Ingredients for lemon butter sauce:

> 1 c. butter, unsalted, melted
> ½ tsp. lemon zest
> 1 Tbs. lemon juice
>   sea salt, to taste
>   ground pepper, to taste

Directions:

1. With large knife, cut stems off artichokes so they sit flat on the plate. While working with one artichoke, place others in a large bowl of water and the lemon juice. This will prevent the artichokes from discoloring.
2. Cut off top ⅓ of artichoke.
3. Clip points off remaining bottom of outer leaves.
4. Repeat with remaining artichokes.
5. In large pot, place 1 to 2 inches water in bottom with sea salt, and steam artichokes for 20 to 30 minutes (depending on their size).

6. Test doneness by pulling one of the leaves out easily.
7. Drain; serve upright with lemon butter sauce or chill and serve with a vinaigrette or flavored mayonnaise.
8. Whisk together all sauce ingredients and serve in small dipping bowls.

Yields: 8 servings.

Crusty Pecan Squash

This is a simple broiled squash. Enjoy.

Ingredients:

1 med. butternut squash, pared, seeded, cut up
1 c. pecans
⅓ c. sugar
½ tsp. cinnamon
2 Tbs. maple syrup

Directions:

1. In large saucepan, cook squash in boiling, salted water until tender; drain.
2. Place pecans in blender container; cover.
3. On low speed, process until coarsely chopped.
4. Empty into small bowl and reserve.
5. Place squash, sugar, and cinnamon into blender; cover.
6. On low speed, process until squash is puréed.
7. Empty into 1-quart, ovenproof casserole.
8. Top with chopped nuts and drizzle with syrup.
9. Place under broiler for 3 to 5 minutes, or until glazed and browned.

Pecan Brown Rice

This is a great brown rice recipe to go with your holiday meal.

Ingredients:

    3   c. brown rice
    2   c. beef broth, and additional water to make 6 c.
    1   Tbs. hot sauce
    1   Tbs. butter
    4   celery ribs, chopped
    1   med. onion, chopped
    2   green onion, chopped with some green
    1½ c. pecans, toasted
       salt and pepper, to taste

Directions:

1. Measure broth, hot sauce, and hot water to make 6 cups of liquid.
2. Bring to boil; add brown rice, cover.
3. Cook 30 to 40 minutes, or until tender.
4. In large skillet, heat butter; add onions and celery, and cook until just limp.
5. Add pecans and toss until well mixed; set aside.
6. Remove from heat until rice is cooked.
7. When rice is done, add celery, onions, and pecans; mix well.
8. Add additional butter if necessary.
9. Taste, and add salt and pepper as necessary.

Did You Know? . . . .

Did you know that during the holidays there are many good deeds waiting to be done by your child and you, together?

Christmas Delights Cookbook
A Collection of Christmas Recipes
Cookbook Delights Holiday Series Book 12

Soups

Table of Contents

Page

African Peanut Soup

This is a thick, hearty soup that is delicious. Serve it topped with plenty of chopped scallions and chopped peanuts.

Ingredients:

2 c. onion, chopped
1 Tbs. canola oil
½ tsp. cayenne pepper
1 tsp. fresh ginger, peeled, grated
1 c. carrots, chopped
2 c. sweet potatoes, chopped
4 c. vegetable stock or water
2 c. tomato juice
1 c. peanut butter, smooth
1 Tbs. sugar
¼ c. scallions, chopped
½ c. peanuts, roasted

Directions:

1. In large pot, sauté onion in oil until translucent.
2. Stir in cayenne and ginger.
3. Add carrots and sauté a couple minutes more.
4. Mix in sweet potatoes and stock.
5. Bring to boil; simmer 15 minutes until vegetables are tender.
6. In blender or food processor, purée vegetables with tomato juice (add some of the cooking liquid if necessary).
7. Return the purée to the pot.
8. Stir in peanut butter until smooth.
9. Check sweetness, and add sugar if necessary.
10. Reheat gently.
11. Add more water, stock, or tomato juice to make a thinner soup if desired.

Apple Butternut Squash Soup

Autumn gardens yield lots of apples and squash; this recipe offers a tasty combination of both.

Ingredients:

4　Tbs. butter, unsalted
2　lg. onions, chopped
2　Tbs. curry powder
1　tsp. chili powder
5　c. chicken stock (homemade or low-sodium canned)
1　lg. butternut squash, peeled, seeded, chopped
3　firm apples,　peeled, cored, diced
½ c. whipping cream
　　fresh parsley or cilantro, chopped, for garnish
　　salt and fresh ground black pepper, to taste

Directions:

1. In heavy skillet, melt butter over medium heat.
2. Add onions and sauté until translucent.
3. Add curry and chili powders.
4. Cook for 5 minutes.
5. Transfer mixture to a soup kettle, and add squash and apples.
6. Add half of the stock and bring to boil.
7. Reduce heat; season with salt and pepper.
8. Simmer 45 minutes to 1 hour, or until squash is tender, stirring occasionally to prevent sticking.
9. Remove from heat, strain soup, and reserve liquid.
10. Place pulp in food processor and pulse until puréed.
11. Return purée to the reserved liquid.
12. Add cream and remaining chicken stock to the soup kettle and bring to a simmer.
13. Ladle into warm bowls; sprinkle with chopped parsley or cilantro and serve warm.

Bacon and Potato Soup

This is a delicious soup flavored with bacon and cheese. It's always popular with guests.

Ingredients:

12 bacon slices, thick
1½ tsp. olive oil
½ c. onion, chopped
⅔ c. carrots, chopped
3   celery stalks, chopped
4   c. chicken broth
4   c. red potatoes, cubed
⅛ tsp. cayenne pepper
1   c. Cheddar cheese, shredded
½ tsp. garlic salt (optional)

Directions:

1. In 3-quart saucepan, cook bacon until crisp.
2. Remove and drain well on paper towels.
3. Discard bacon grease and wipe pan with paper towel.
4. Add oil to saucepan; add onion, carrot, and celery.
5. Sauté 3 to 4 minutes, or until onion is soft, but not brown.
6. Stir in chicken broth, potatoes, and pepper.
7. Bring to boil.
8. Reduce heat.
9. Simmer, covered, until potatoes are tender.
10. Stir in cheese, heating just until melted.
11. Do not boil.
12. Chop bacon and add to soup.
13. Adjust seasoning to taste by adding garlic salt, if desired.

Beef Stew

This is the old-fashioned beef stew my grandmother used to make, and my family enjoys it just as it is. Feel free to modify it by adding other vegetables of your preference.

Ingredients:

1 lb. beef stew meat, cut into ½-inch pieces
1 med. onion, cut into eighths
1 pkg. baby carrots (8 oz.), cut up
1 can tomatoes, diced tomatoes, undrained
1 can condensed beef broth
1 can tomato sauce (8 oz.)
⅓ c. flour
1 Tbs. hot sauce
1 Tbs. sugar
1 tsp. dried marjoram leaves
¼ tsp. pepper
12 med. potatoes, cut into fourths
2 c. mushrooms, sliced

Directions:

1. Preheat oven to 325 degrees F.
2. In 4-quart Dutch oven, mix all ingredients except potatoes and mushrooms together.
3. Cover and bake 2 hours, stirring once.
4. Stir in potatoes and mushrooms.
5. Cover and bake 1 to 1½ hours, or until beef and vegetables are tender; stir well.
6. Note: This may be cooked in a crock-pot. Cover; cook on low heat setting 8 to 9 hours, or until vegetables are tender.
7. Stir well.

Did You Know?...
Did you know one of the most precious gifts is time?

Beer Cheese Soup

This soup is unique in its blend of beer and cheese flavors.

Ingredients:

2 Tbs. butter
¼ c. onion, chopped
½ c. celery, thinly sliced
2 Tbs. flour
¼ tsp. pepper
¼ tsp. ground mustard
1 bottle beer or non-alcoholic beer (12 oz.)
1 c. milk
2 c. Cheddar cheese, shredded
popped popcorn, if desired
paprika (optional)

Directions:

1. Melt butter in 2-quart saucepan over medium heat.
2. Cook onion and celery in butter about 2 minutes, stirring occasionally, until tender.
3. Stir in flour, pepper, and mustard.
4. Stir in beer and milk.
5. Heat to boiling over medium heat, stirring constantly.
6. Boil and stir 1 minute; reduce heat to low.
7. Gradually stir in cheese.
8. Heat over low heat, stirring constantly, just until cheese is melted.
9. Sprinkle each serving with popcorn.
10. You may substitute a 10½-ounce can of condensed chicken broth for the beer, if desired.
11. Serve topped with paprika, if desired.
12. Serve with your favorite buns or bread.

Black Bean Onion Soup

My husband especially loves black bean soup. This soup is rich and full of flavor, especially with the Cheddar cheese.

Ingredients:

- 2   med. onions, chopped
- 2   garlic cloves, minced
- 1   Tbs. canola oil
- 6   c. black beans, cooked
- 7   c. water
- 1½ c. green pepper, chopped
-     salt and pepper, to taste
-     sharp Cheddar cheese, shredded, to taste
-     whole wheat bread or crackers

Directions:

1. In skillet over medium heat, sauté onion and garlic in oil until soft, 5 to 7 minutes.
2. Combine onion and garlic in large pot with beans and water.
3. Bring to boil.
4. Add green pepper.
5. Reduce heat and simmer 10 minutes.
6. Allow to cool slightly.
7. Purée half of soup in a blender.
8. Return mixture from blender to pot and heat to serving temperature.
9. Top with cheese.
10. Serve with whole wheat bread or crackers.

Did You Know? . . . .

Did you know another gift you can give your children is to engage them in cultural, religious, and traditional activities throughout the Christmas season?

Karen's Clam Corn Chowder

This is one of our favorites and is always a hit with guests when it's cold outside.

Ingredients:

6 slices crisp bacon, crumbled
1 med. onion, chopped
¼ c. butter
3 cans clams, chopped (8 oz.), with juice
1 c. fresh corn on the cob
2 c. diced potatoes
½ tsp. salt
¼ tsp. fresh pepper
2 c. heavy cream
2 Tbs. flour

Directions:

1. In Dutch oven, sauté chopped onion in butter, sprinkle 2 tablespoons flour over melted butter, and stir.
2. Add everything else except the flour.
3. In measuring cup, mix flour with a little bit of warm water to dissolve it.
4. Add mixture to pot and bring just to boiling.
5. Cover and simmer for 30 minutes.
6. If you want a thicker base, add a little more flour.
7. Serve with oyster crackers, fresh bread, and a salad.

Did You Know? . . . .

Did you know that sharing with your children the gift of giving is the most precious gift you can give them? There are books to be read to blind children and adults, food to be served at shelters on Christmas Eve and Christmas day, toys to be delivered to orphanages and hospices, and songs to be sung in nursing homes.

Lobster Bisque

Try this wonderful, thicker, creamy soup, just full of flavor, with any meal.

Ingredients:

2 cans lobster meat (6 oz. ea.)
½ c. onion, chopped
¾ c. butter
¾ c. flour, sifted
2 cans condensed chicken broth (10½ oz. ea.)
¾ c. dry sherry
3 c. light cream
2 Tbs. tomato paste
½ tsp. salt
    dash of pepper

Directions:

1. Drain lobster, removing any cartilage.
2. Set aside several large pieces for garnish, then dice remainder.
3. In large saucepan, sauté onion in butter until soft.
4. Stir in flour; cook, stirring constantly, until bubbly.
5. Stir in chicken broth; continue cooking and stirring until mixture thickens and boils for 1 minute.
6. Stir in diced lobster and sherry.
7. Cover and simmer 20 minutes.
8. Blend in cream, tomato paste, salt, and pepper.
9. Heat slowly just until hot.
10. Ladle into a tureen; float saved pieces of lobster on top.

Yields: 8 servings.

Cheddar Vegetable Chowder

This is a tasty vegetable chowder recipe with potatoes, Cheddar cheese, carrots, and other vegetables and seasonings.

Ingredients:

¼ c. butter
1 c. carrots, thinly sliced
1 c. potatoes, diced
1 c. green beans, sliced
½ c. onion, chopped
½ c. celery, thinly sliced
2 Tbs. green bell pepper, finely chopped
2 Tbs. red bell pepper, finely chopped
3 Tbs. cornstarch
½ tsp. salt, or to taste
1 tsp. dry mustard
4 c. chicken broth
1 Tbs. hot sauce
1 c. Cheddar cheese, coarsely shredded

Directions:

1. In large saucepan or Dutch oven, over medium heat, melt butter.
2. Add carrots, potatoes, green beans, onion, celery, and bell peppers.
3. Sauté 5 minutes, stirring constantly.
4. In small bowl, combine cornstarch with salt and dry mustard.
5. Gradually stir in chicken broth and hot sauce until smooth.
6. Add to vegetable mixture and bring to boil, stirring constantly.
7. Boil 1 minute longer.

8. Reduce heat, cover, and simmer 30 minutes, or until vegetables are tender.
9. Add cheese and stir until melted.
10. Taste and adjust seasoning.

Yields: 6 servings.

Ham and Barley Soup

This is a delicious soup that is hearty and satisfying. Serve it with homemade biscuits, hot from the oven.

Ingredients:

4   lg. celery stalks
4   lg. carrots
1   med. onion
12 c. water
2   c. ham
1   c. barley
1   can tomatoes, (16 oz.), stewed or crushed
9   oz. green beans, frozen Italian
    salt and pepper, to taste

Directions:

1. Cut celery into ¼-inch slices, cut carrots into pieces, and dice onions.
2. In Dutch oven, over medium-high heat, place cut vegetables, water, ham, barley, salt, and pepper.
3. Cover and simmer for 1½ hours.
4. Skim any fat from soup.
5. Add tomatoes and beans; heat to boiling.
6. Cover and simmer on low 10 minutes.

Yields: 10 servings.

Turkey Noodle Soup

My mom and aunts always made homemade noodles when I was growing up. I can remember going to their home and seeing a sheet or table cloth on their dining table or bed with homemade noodles drying on it.

Ingredients for homemade noodles:

  7 c. flour
  5 lg. eggs
  1 c. water
  1 tsp. salt

Ingredients for soup:

  1 c. celery, chopped
  1 c. onion, chopped
  ¼ c. butter
  12 c. water
  1 c. carrots, diced
  3 Tbs. chicken bouillon
  ½ tsp. marjoram leaves
  ¼ tsp. pepper
  1 bay leaf
  6 oz. homemade noodles (recipe above)
  4 c. leftover turkey, cooked, diced
  1 Tbs. parsley, chopped

Directions for homemade noodles:

  1. In large bowl, beat eggs, salt, and water.
  2. Add flour slowly until a ball is formed.
  3. Mix in remaining flour by hand, and knead until dough is smooth.
  4. Cover dough with a bowl, and let rest 10 minutes before rolling out.

5. Divide dough into two balls.
6. Place one ball on a floured surface, and flatten with your hand into an oblong about 1-inch thick.
7. Using a heavy rolling pin, start at one end of the oblong and roll it out lengthwise away from you.
8. Turn the dough often, rolling it first on one side, then on the other, flouring the surface and rolling pin occasionally, until $1/16$-inch thick.
9. Roll up the dough tightly into a long roll.
10. With a sharp knife, cut into rolls about ¼-inch thick.
11. Separate and unroll the slices.
12. Spread the noodles on a clean tablecloth, tossing them gently with fingers to unfold them.
13. Let the noodles dry completely.
14. Follow the same procedure with remaining dough.
15. Note: The extra noodles freeze beautifully.

Directions for soup:

1. In large Dutch oven, cook celery and onion in butter until tender.
2. Add remaining ingredients except noodles and parsley.
3. Bring to boil, and reduce heat.
4. Simmer, covered for 30 minutes.
5. Remove bay leaf, and add noodles and parsley.
6. Cook 10 minutes longer, or until noodles are tender, stirring occasionally.

Did You Know?

Did you know you can create family traditions that involve giving back to the community? Shopping for extra groceries to give to a food bank, volunteering at a shelter, or donating toys are all ways that even young children can get involved in to help others.

Turkey Green Chili

Poblano and jalapeno chilies, tomatillos, and cilantro account for this recipe's title.

Ingredients:

1½ lb. poblano chilies
2   Tbs. olive oil
½   lb. pork, chicken, or turkey chorizo sausages, casings removed
3   c. onions, chopped
6   lg. garlic cloves, chopped
2   Tbs. chili powder
1   tsp. ground cumin
5   lb. turkey thighs with bones, skinned, deboned, cubed
2   c. chicken broth
12 oz. fresh tomatillos, husked, rinsed, chopped
1   c. canned tomatoes, drained, diced
½   c. fresh cilantro stems, chopped
2   Tbs. fresh lime juice
1   Tbs. jalapeno chili with seeds, chopped

Directions:

1. Char poblanos directly over gas flame or in broiler until blackened on all sides.
2. Enclose in plastic bag; let stand 10 minutes.
3. Peel, seed, and chop poblanos.
4. In large saucepan, over medium heat, heat oil.
5. Add chorizo; sauté 5 minutes, or until cooked through, breaking up with back of fork.
6. Add onions and garlic.
7. Cover and cook 10 minutes.
8. Mix in chili powder and cumin.
9. Sprinkle turkey with salt and pepper.
10. Add to saucepan; stir.
11. Add broth and next 5 ingredients.
12. Mix in roasted poblanos.
13. Bring chili to boil, stirring occasionally.
14. Reduce heat to medium-low; simmer, uncovered, 45 minutes, or until turkey is tender.

Yields: 8 servings.

Christmas Delights Cookbook
A Collection of Christmas Recipes
Cookbook Delights Holiday Series Book 12

Wines and Spirits

Table of Contents

Page

About Cooking with Alcohol

Some recipes in this cookbook contain, among other ingredients, liquors. It is for the purpose of obtaining desired flavor and achieving culinary appreciation and not to be abused in any way. In cooking and baking, alcohol evaporates and only the flavor may be enjoyed. When mixed in cold, however, such as in desserts, caution must be exercised. These recipes are intended for people who may consume small amounts of alcohol in a responsible and safe manner.

I live in Washington State and we are proud of our wine production. Washington State is rapidly gaining prestige as a premier wine producer. Do enjoy the art of wine tasting and enjoy the completeness and uniqueness of each wine. It is an art to enjoy and savor in moderation.

If consumption of even small amounts of alcoholic ingredients presents a problem, in whatever form, please substitute coffee flavor syrups, found in coffee sections of supermarkets. For example, instead of Southern Comfort liqueur, substitute with Irish Cream or Amaretto Syrup.

Karen Jean Matsko Hood

Raspberry Wine Punch

This is an easy-to-make wine punch.

Ingredients:

½ c. raspberry claret
1 liter ginger ale
1 bottle sauterne
1 bottle dry champagne

Directions:

1. All ingredients must be well chilled.
2. Mix and serve with ice ring and mint leaves.

Christmas Glogg

This traditional Danish Christmas drink will warm your heart and your taste buds.

Ingredients:

1-2 cinnamon sticks
5   whole cloves
4   whole allspice
3   cardamom pods
1   pinch ginger, freshly grated
½   c. raw sugar, or to taste
2-3 Tbs. Madeira (optional)
⅓   c. raisins
2   c. water
¼   tsp. orange extract
¼   tsp. lemon extract
2   tsp. orange peel, grated
2   tsp. lemon peel, grated
1   bottle red wine
¼   c. almonds, slivered, for serving
¼   c. vodka (optional, for serving)

Directions:

1. In large saucepan, stir all ingredients together except wine, almonds, and vodka.
2. Simmer 1 hour; turn off heat and let mixture sit overnight.
3. When ready to serve, pour a bottle of red wine into the mixture, and slowly let it come to a simmer.
4. Do not let the drink get even close to boiling.
5. Stir every now and then, and taste with a spoon whenever you feel like it.
6. To serve, put a few slivered almonds in the bottom of red wine glasses, and pour the glogg on top.
7. Your whole house will smell beautiful. Enjoy.

Frozen Margarita

This traditional frozen margarita is always enjoyed.

Ingredients:

    2 tsp. coarse salt
    1 lime wedge
    3 oz. white tequila
    1 oz. triple sec
    2 oz. lime juice
    1 c. ice, crushed

Directions:

1. Place salt in a saucer.
2. Rub rim of cocktail glass with lime wedge and dip glass in salt to coat rim thoroughly, reserve lime.
3. Pour tequila, triple sec, lime juice, and ice into blender.
4. Blend well at high speed.
5. Pour into a cocktail glass.

Cherry Garcia

Try this delicious and tropical, refreshing drink during your holiday gathering.

Ingredients:

    2 oz. cherry ice cream
    1 oz. maraschino cherries and juice
    1 oz. light rum (optional)
    1 oz. coconut syrup
    ½ oz. pineapple juice
    ½ oz. cream
    1 maraschino cherry with stem, for garnishment crushed ice

Directions:

1. In blender container, combine all ingredients except ice and maraschino cherry with stem.
2. Fill with ice to equal 11 ounces.
3. Blend until smooth.
4. Pour into tall 12-ounce glass, garnish with cherry, and serve with a straw.

Hazelnut Truffles Cocktail

Chocolate and hazelnut is a match made in heaven. These flavors combine for an elegant ending to your holiday dinner party.

Ingredients:

6 oz. (¾ c.) Frangelico
6 oz. (¾ c.) Godiva liqueur
   shaved milk chocolate or semi-sweet chocolate

Directions:

1. Dip edges of 4 martini glasses in the liqueurs, and rim them with shaved chocolate.
2. In small spouted or lipped-rim saucepan, combine liqueurs.
3. Heat over medium to high heat until warm, but not hot.
4. Pour into the chocolate-rimmed martini glasses, being careful not to disturb the chocolate, and serve.
5. Note: If spouted or lipped-rim pan is not available, pour the warm liqueur into the martini glasses through a funnel.

Yields: 4 servings.

Quick Kahlua

This is so easy and quick to make, and the more months it sits in a dark cupboard, the better it tastes.

Ingredients:

- 4 c. sugar
- 4 c. hot water
- ¼ c. instant coffee
- 2 Tbs. plus 2 tsp. pure vanilla extract
- 1 bottle (2 qt.) vodka

Directions:

1. In large saucepan, mix sugar, hot water, instant coffee, and bring to simmer.
2. Cover and simmer for 1½ hours.
3. Remove from heat and cool.
4. Mix in vanilla.
5. Add vodka.
6. Place in bottles and store in cool, dark cupboard.

Mimosa

Mimosas are a perfect choice for your holiday brunch or dinner.

Ingredients:

- 3 oz. champagne, chilled
- 3 oz. orange juice
- 1 dash Grand Marnier

Directions:

1. Pour orange juice into a large, chilled wine glass.
2. Slowly pour in the champagne, stirring gently.
3. Top with a dash of Grand Marnier.

Hot Apple Rum Cider

Hot cider with spices and rum is perfect on a cold day.

Ingredients:

    2   qt. apple cider, unsweetened
    1   can frozen orange juice concentrate (6 oz.), thawed
    ¼   c. lemon juice
    ¼   c. honey
    2   cinnamon sticks
    ¼   tsp. whole cloves
    1   tsp. coriander seeds
    1   whole nutmeg
    1¼ c. dark rum or brandy
         cinnamon sticks, for garnish
         orange slices, for garnish

Directions:

1. In large saucepan, combine cider, juices, honey, and spices; cook over medium heat until thoroughly heated, stirring frequently.
2. Reduce heat; simmer 15 minutes.
3. Remove and discard cinnamon sticks, cloves, coriander seeds, and nutmeg, using a slotted spoon.
4. Stir in rum; cook over medium heat until thoroughly heated. Do not boil.
5. Pour into mugs. If desired, garnish with cinnamon sticks and orange slices.
6. Extra cider or apple punch can be refrigerated for a week in airtight container.

Yields: 8 to 10 servings.

Did You Know? . . .

Did you know that if you talk with your kids about the roots of your family's traditions, you share a deeper gift?

Hot Buttered Rum Mix

This is an old recipe from Montana I make for holiday gatherings and it is always a hit. It is guaranteed to get rid of a winter chill. I make half this recipe, and the leftover batter keeps in the freezer all winter for unexpected guests.

Ingredients:

- 1 qt. vanilla ice cream
- 1 lb. powdered sugar
- 1 lb. brown sugar
- 1 lb. butter (4 cubes)
- 1 tsp. cinnamon
- 1 tsp. nutmeg
- ⅛ tsp. allspice or cloves
  rum

Directions:

1. In large bowl, with electric mixer, beat all ingredients together except the rum.
2. Scoop into airtight container and store in freezer.
3. Serve in warmed cups with 1 heaping teaspoon of mix, 1 jigger of rum, and hot water to the top.
4. Garnish with a cinnamon stick and nutmeg, if desired.
5. Note: Brandy is an excellent substitute for the rum in this drink.
6. Don't want alcohol? Substitute evaporated milk for rum when serving.
7. An excellent variation for serving this mix is to put 1 teaspoon of this mix into a hot cup of coffee with a shot of kahlua.

Did You Know? . . .

Did you know a sparkle in a child's eyes is contagious?

Hot Mulled Wine

Wine is not often consumed hot anymore, but at one time it was a heartening treat in the winter.

Ingredients:

- 1 bottle red wine
- 12 cloves
- 2 cinnamon sticks
- 2 Tbs. sugar
- rind of 1 lemon

Directions:

1. Add all ingredients to a saucepan, and steep gently over medium heat until hot.
2. Avoid boiling the mixture.
3. Serve in festive mugs and enjoy.

Raspberry Daiquiri

This makes a refreshing version of the daiquiri drink.

Ingredients:

- 1¼ oz. white rum
- ¾ c. raspberries
- 1 Tbs. simple syrup (½ water, ½ sugar)
- 1½ c. ice
- ¼ c. orange juice

Directions:

1. Blend all ingredients in blender until smooth.
2. Serve in tall glass, and garnish with an orange slice and raspberry, if desired.

Raspberry Eggnog

My family enjoys eggnog, and this makes a colorful drink to enjoy over the holidays or year round.

Ingredients:

2 c. raspberries
2 c. water
4 eggs
⅔ c. sugar or honey
1 Tbs. vanilla extract
1 tsp. nutmeg
2 c. heavy cream (1 pt.)
1 c. brandy or dark rum (optional)

Directions:

1. In medium saucepan, mix raspberries and water.
2. Boil gently for 15 minutes.
3. Press mixture through a fine strainer.
4. Pour into a bowl and chill.
5. Beat eggs into raspberry purée until smooth.
6. Beat in sugar, vanilla, and nutmeg.
7. Gradually beat in heavy cream and brandy.
8. Chill until ready to serve.
9. Stir again before serving in punch cups.

Yields: 6 servings.

Sangria

This makes a nice punch bowl for your holiday parties.

Ingredients:

1 orange, cut in half, ½ thinly sliced, ½ juiced
1 lemon, thinly sliced

1 bottle dry white wine
2 Tbs. sugar
1 oz. brandy
1 oz. Cointreau
2 c. ice cubes
1 c. club soda

Directions:

1. In punch bowl, combine orange and lemon slices, orange juice, wine, sugar, brandy, and Cointreau.
2. Chill.
3. To serve, add ice and club soda; stir gently.

Sleepless in Seattle

This drink is for those of you who enjoy coffee with chocolate and cherry.

Ingredients:

1 oz. maraschino cherry juice
1 oz. chocolate syrup
1 oz. espresso
6 oz. light cream or milk
1 oz. coffee-flavored liqueur
1 maraschino cherry with stem, drained
   whipped cream, for garnish

Directions:

1. In small saucepan, combine cherry juice, chocolate syrup, and espresso.
2. Heat to boiling, stirring occasionally.
3. Reduce heat, stir in cream, and heat to scalding.
4. Serve in mug topped with dollop of whipped cream, liqueur, and a maraschino cherry.

Strawberry Kiss

This is a pleasing tropical blend with additional flavors of strawberries and peaches.

Ingredients:

    1 oz. strawberry liqueur
    1 oz. peach schnapps
    1 oz. orange juice
    1 oz. pineapple juice
    1 dash grenadine
    1 splash cream
      strawberry wedge

Directions:

1. Pour alcohol first, then add juices, followed by grenadine and cream.
2. Garnish with strawberry wedge.

Strawberry-Laced Punch

This punch provides a festive color and delicious flavors to your special gathering.

Ingredients:

    ½ c. vodka
    5 c. ice cubes
    5 c. strawberry juice
    1 c. white wine
    1 c. lime juice
    3 c. peach juice
    1 c. rum

Directions:

1. Mix fruit juices in bowl and place in blender with ice cubes; blend.
2. When slushy mixture is complete, stir in alcohol, and shake until completely mixed.
3. Place mixture in punch bowl.

Strawberry Liqueur

This is a great tasting, easy-to-make strawberry liqueur and makes a great gift.

Ingredients:

1   pt. strawberries
4   lemons
1½ c. kouri-zatou (rock sugar)
1   bottle white liquor (or vodka)

Directions:

1. Wash strawberries and drain well.
2. Cut peels from lemons, removing as much of white as possible.
3. Cut lemons into 2 or 3 pieces.
4. Pour liquor into large clean glass jar or bottle.
5. Remove strawberry stems, dropping the hulled berries into the jar.
6. Add lemons and rock sugar.
7. Seal jar and leave in cool, dark place for 2 months, or until liqueur turns nice and red.
8. Strain to remove fruit and transfer to clean bottles.

Did You Know? . . .

Did you know the "Twelve Days of Christmas" refers to the time taken by the Three Wise Men (the Magi) to reach Bethlehem to see the babe in the manger, Jesus?

Wassail

Wassail was originally not a drink, but a practice of caroling. In Merry Old England carolers would bring a cup with them, and, as they sang before the homes of wealthy citizens, their mugs would be filled with a hot spiced ale, often with a roasted apple slice floating in it.

Ingredients:

1 bottle burgundy or claret wine
6 eggs
½ c. water
¼ tsp. nutmeg
2 cloves
½ tsp. ginger
½ tsp. mace
½ tsp. allspice
½ tsp. cinnamon
2 c. sugar
6 apples, baked

Directions:

1. Heat the bottle of red wine.
2. Meanwhile separate the eggs.
3. Beat the yokes and whites separately, then fold both together. The egg whites should be stiff.
4. Put spices in water and heat for a few minutes to release flavor.
5. Pour all into a punch bowl along with baked apples.
6. Serve warm.

Did You Know? ...

Did you know that telling kids the religious story of Christmas at an early age, and retelling it as they grow, will help them remember the deeper meaning of the holiday?

Christmas Celebrations and Winter Festivals

Christmas is celebrated all over the world. This is the most important and the happiest festival of the Christians. Other communities also look upon it as a festival of goodwill and greetings.

Shops and homes take on a festive air. Streets and markets come alive with festival wares. In the festivities there are dances, songs, Christmas trees, and decorations everywhere you look. Santa Claus is moving through the streets with his glittering, colorful robes, glowing long white beard, as he shakes hands with children in the streets. Families get together around sparkling Christmas trees from whose branches hang numerous lovely gifts. Christmas raises everyone's spirits. It is a hue of joy, celebration, and festivity.

Children roll snow and pack it into snowmen and ice sculptures. There are awesome snow and ice sculptures everywhere there's snow. But lately, simple designs are giving way to some amazing creations. More competitions in snow or ice carving are taking place in the United States and many other countries. In fact, serious carvers are traveling to distant corners of the earth to enter these winter festivals and contests.

A giant snow maze was built for a winter festival in Winnipeg, a city in Manitoba, Canada. St. Paul, Minnesota's colorfully lit ice castle brightens up their night sky. It was built for the city's Winter Carnival. The castle stands nearly 16 stories high, as tall as an office building, and is made of 20,000 blocks of ice.

Did You Know?....

Did you know that if you don't have any castor sugar on hand, you can make your own by grinding granulated sugar for a couple of minutes in a food processor?

Christmas Tree Associations

The National Christmas Tree Association
16020 Swingley Ridge Road, Suite 300
Chesterfield, MO 63017
Phone: (636) 449-5070
Fax: (636) 449-5051
Email: info@realchristmastrees.org

State and Regional Association Contacts

The National Christmas Tree Association works closely with many state and regional Christmas tree associations. If you are looking for a local contact for information, we suggest you contact a Christmas tree association in your immediate area. If you are unable to find an association in your area, you may contact the National Christmas Tree Association listed above.

Associations in the Northwest

Pacific Northwest
Bryan Ostlund
P.O. Box 3366
Salem, OR 97302
Business Phone: (503) 364-2942
Fax: (503) 581-6819
Website: www.nwtrees.com
Email: bryan@ostlund.com

Inland Empire
Allen Huckaba
8022 E. Greenbluff Road
Colbert, WA 99005-9561
Business Phone: (509) 238-6742
Website: www.iecta.org
Email: ehuckaba@aol.com

U.S. and Metric Measurement Charts

Here are some measurement equivalents to help you with exchanges. There was a time when many people thought the entire world would convert to the metric scale. While most of the world has, America still has not. Metric conversions in cooking are vitally important to preparing a tasty recipe. Here are simple conversion tables that should come in handy.

U.S. Measurement Equivalents

A few grains/pinch/dash, (dry) = Less than ⅛ teaspoon
A dash (liquid) = A few drops
3 teaspoons = 1 tablespoon
½ tablespoon = 1½ teaspoons
1 tablespoon = 3 teaspoons
2 tablespoons = 1 fluid ounce
4 tablespoons = ¼ cup
5⅓ tablespoons = ⅓ cup
8 tablespoons = ½ cup
8 tablespoons = 4 fluid ounces
10⅔ tablespoons = ⅔ cup
12 tablespoons = ¾ cup
16 tablespoons = 1 cup
16 tablespoons = 8 fluid ounces
⅛ cup = 2 tablespoons
¼ cup = 4 tablespoons
¼ cup = 2 fluid ounces
⅓ cup = 5 tablespoons plus 1 teaspoon
½ cup = 8 tablespoons
1 cup = 16 tablespoons
1 cup = 8 fluid ounces
1 cup = ½ pint
2 cups = 1 pint
2 pints = 1 quart
4 quarts (liquid) = 1 gallon
8 quarts (dry) = 1 peck
4 pecks (dry) = 1 bushel
1 kilogram = approximately 2 pounds
1 liter=approximately 4 cups or 1quart

Approximate Metric Equivalents by Volume

U.S.	Metric
¼ cup	= 60 milliliters
½ cup	= 120 milliliters
1 cup	= 230 milliliters
1¼ cups	= 300 milliliters
1½ cups	= 360 milliliters
2 cups	= 460 milliliters
2½ cups	= 600 milliliters
3 cups	= 700 milliliters
4 cups (1 quart)	= .95 liter
1.06 quarts	= 1 liter
4 quarts (1 gallon)	= 3.8 liters

Approximate Metric Equivalents by Weight

U.S.	Metric
¼ ounce	= 7 grams
½ ounce	= 14 grams
1 ounce	= 28 grams
1¼ ounces	= 35 grams
1½ ounces	= 40 grams
2½ ounces	= 70 grams
4 ounces	= 112 grams
5 ounces	= 140 grams
8 ounces	= 228 grams
10 ounces	= 280 grams
15 ounces	= 425 grams
16 ounces (1 pound)	= 454 grams

Glossary

Aerate: A synonym for sift; to pass ingredients through a fine-mesh device to break up large pieces and incorporate air into ingredients to make them lighter.

Al dente: "To the tooth," in Italian. The pasta is cooked just enough to maintain a firm, chewy texture.

Baste: To brush or spoon liquid fat or juices over meat during roasting to add flavor and prevent drying out.

Bias-slice: To slice a food crosswise at a 45-degree angle.

Bind: To thicken a sauce or hot liquid by stirring in ingredients such as eggs, flour, butter, or cream until it holds together.

Blackened: Popular Cajun-style cooking method. Seasoned foods are cooked over high heat in a super-heated heavy skillet until charred.

Blanch: To scald, as in vegetables being prepared for freezing; as in almonds so as to remove skins.

Blend: To mix or fold two or more ingredients together to obtain equal distribution throughout the mixture.

Braise: To brown meat in oil or other fat and then cook slowly in liquid. The effect of braising is to tenderize the meat.

Bread: To coat food with crumbs (usually with soft or dry bread crumbs), sometimes seasoned.

Brown: To quickly sauté, broil, or grill either at the beginning or at the end of meal preparation, often to enhance flavor, texture, or eye appeal.

Brush: To use a pastry brush to coat a food such as meat or pastry with melted butter, glaze, or other liquid.

Butterfly: To cut open a food such as pork chops down the center without cutting all the way through, and then spread apart.

Caramelization: Browning sugar over a flame, with or without the addition of some water to aid the process. The temperature range in which sugar caramelizes is approximately 320 to 360 degrees F.

Clarify: To remove impurities from butter or stock by heating the liquid, then straining or skimming it.

Coddle: A cooking method in which foods (such as eggs) are put in separate containers and placed in a pan of simmering water for slow, gentle cooking.

Confit: To slowly cook pieces of meat in their own gently rendered fat.

Core: To remove the inedible center of fruits such as pineapples.

Cream: To beat vegetable shortening, butter, or margarine, with or without sugar, until light and fluffy. This process traps in air bubbles, later used to create height in cookies and cakes.

Crimp: To create a decorative edge on a pie crust. On a double pie crust, this also seals the edges together.

Curd: A custard-like pie or tart filling flavored with juice and zest of citrus fruit, usually lemon, although lime and orange may also be used.

Curdle: To cause semisolid pieces of coagulated protein to develop in food, usually as a result of the addition of an acid substance, or the overheating of milk or egg-based sauces.

Custard: A mixture of beaten egg, milk, and possibly other ingredients such as sweet or savory flavorings, which are cooked with gentle heat, often in a water bath or double boiler. As pie filling, the custard is frequently cooked and chilled before being layered into a baked crust.

Deglaze: To add liquid to a pan in which foods have been fried or roasted, in order to dissolve the caramelized juices stuck to the bottom of the pan.

Dot: To sprinkle food with small bits of an ingredient such as butter to allow for even melting.

Dredge: To sprinkle lightly and evenly with sugar or flour. A dredger has holes pierced on the lid to sprinkle evenly.

Drippings: The liquids left in the bottom of a roasting or frying pan after meat is cooked. Drippings are generally used for gravies and sauces.

Drizzle: To pour a liquid such as a sweet glaze or melted butter in a slow, light trickle over food.

Dust: To sprinkle food lightly with spices, sugar, or flour for a light coating.

Egg Wash: A mixture of beaten eggs (yolks, whites, or whole eggs) with either milk or water. Used to coat cookies and other baked goods to give them a shine when baked.

Emulsion: A mixture of liquids, one being a fat or oil and the other being water based so that tiny globules of one are suspended in the other. This may involve the use of stabilizers, such as egg or custard. Emulsions may be temporary or permanent.

Entrée: A French term that originally referred to the first course of a meal, served after the soup and before the meat courses. In the United States, it refers to the main dish of a meal.

Fillet: To remove the bones from meat or fish for cooking.

Filter: To remove lumps, excess liquid, or impurities by passing through paper or cheesecloth.

Firm-Ball Stage: In candy making, the point at which boiling syrup dropped in cold water forms a ball that is compact yet gives slightly to the touch.

Flambé: To ignite a sauce or other liquid so that it flames.

Flan: An open pie filled with sweet or savory ingredients; also, a Spanish dessert of baked custard covered with caramel.

Flute: To create a decorative scalloped or undulating edge on a pie crust or other pastry.

Fricassee: Usually a stew in which the meat is cut up, lightly cooked in butter, and then simmered in liquid until done.

Frizzle: To cook thin slices of meat in hot oil until crisp and slightly curly.

Ganache: A rich chocolate filling or coating made with chocolate, vegetable shortening, and possibly heavy cream. It can coat cakes or cookies, and be used as a filling for truffles.

Glaze: A liquid that gives an item a shiny surface. Examples are fruit jams that have been heated or chocolate thinned with melted vegetable shortening. Also, to cover a food with such a liquid.

Gratin: To bind together or combine food with a liquid such as cream, milk, béchamel sauce, or tomato sauce, in a shallow dish. The mixture is then baked until cooked and set.

Hard-Ball Stage: In candy making, the point at which syrup has cooked long enough to form a solid ball in cold water.

Hull (also husk): To remove the leafy parts of soft fruits, such as strawberries or blackberries.

Infusion: To extract flavors by soaking them in liquid heated in a covered pan. The term also refers to the liquid resulting from this process.

Jerk or Jamaican Jerk Seasoning: A dry mixture of various spices such as chilies, thyme, garlic, onions, and cinnamon or cloves used to season meats such as chicken or pork.

Julienne: To cut into long, thin strips.

Jus: The natural juices released by roasting meats.

Larding: To inset strips of fat into pieces of meat, so that the braised meat stays moist and juicy.

Marble: To gently swirl one food into another.

Marinate: To combine food with aromatic ingredients to add flavor.

Meringue: Egg whites beaten until they are stiff, then sweetened. It can be used as the topping for pies or baked as cookies.

Mull: To slowly heat cider with spices and sugar.

Parboil: To partly cook in a boiling liquid.

Peaks: The mounds made in a mixture. For example, egg white that has been whipped to stiffness. Peaks are "stiff" if they stay upright or "soft" if they curl over.

Pesto: A sauce usually made of fresh basil, garlic, olive oil, pine nuts, and cheese. The ingredients are finely chopped and then mixed, uncooked, with pasta. Generally, the term refers to any uncooked sauce made of finely chopped herbs and nuts.

Pipe: To force a semisoft food through a bag (either a pastry bag or a plastic bag with one corner cut off) to decorate food.

Pressure Cooking: To cook using steam trapped under a locked lid to produce high temperatures and achieve fast cooking time.

Purée: To mash or sieve food into a thick liquid.

Ramekin: A small baking dish used for individual servings of sweet and savory dishes.

Reduce: To cook liquids down so that some of the water evaporates.

Refresh: To pour cold water over freshly cooked vegetables to prevent further cooking and to retain color.

Roux: A cooked paste usually made from flour and butter used to thicken sauces.

Sauté: To cook foods quickly in a small amount of oil in a skillet or sauté pan over direct heat.

Scald: To heat a liquid, usually a dairy product, until it almost boils.

Sear: To seal in a meat's juices by cooking it quickly using very high heat.

Seize: To form a thick, lumpy mass when melted (usually applies to chocolate).

Sift: To remove large lumps from a dry ingredient such as flour or confectioners' sugar by passing it through a fine mesh. This process also incorporates air into the ingredients, making them lighter.

Simmer: To cook food in a liquid at a low enough temperature that small bubbles begin to break the surface.

Steam: To cook over boiling water in a covered pan, this method keeps foods' shape, texture, and nutritional value intact better than methods such as boiling.

Steep: To soak dry ingredients (tea leaves, ground coffee, herbs, spices, etc.) in liquid until the flavor is infused into the liquid.

Stewing: To brown small pieces of meat, poultry, or fish, then simmer them with vegetables or other ingredients in enough liquid to cover them, usually in a closed pot on the stove, in the oven, or with a slow cooker.

Thin: To reduce a mixture's thickness with the addition of more liquid.

Truss: To use string, skewers, or pins to hold together a food to maintain its shape while it cooks (usually applied to meat or poultry).

Unleavened: Baked goods that contain no agents to give them volume, such as baking powder, baking soda, or yeast.

Vinaigrette: A general term referring to any sauce made with vinegar, oil, and seasonings.

Zest: The thin, brightly colored outer part of the rind of citrus fruits. It contains volatile oils, used as a flavoring.

Recipe Index of Christmas Delights

315

Reader Feedback Form

Dear Reader,

We are very interested in what our readers think. Please fill in the form below and return it to:

Whispering Pine Press International, Inc.
c/o Christmas Delights Cookbook
P.O. Box 214, Spokane Valley, WA 99037-0214
Phone: (509) 928-8700 | Fax: (509) 922-9949
Email: sales@whisperingpinepress.com
Publisher Websites: www.WhisperingPinePress.com
www.WhisperingPinePressBookstore.com
Blog: www.WhisperingPinePressBlog.com

Name: _____

Address: _____

City, St., Zip: _____

Phone/Fax: (____) _____ / (____) _____

Email: _____

Comments/Suggestions: _____

_____

_____

_____

_____

A great deal of care and attention has been exercised in the creation of this book. Designing a great cookbook that is original, fun, and easy to use has been a job that required many hours of diligence, creativity, and research. Although we strive to make this book completely error free, errors and discrepancies may not be completely excluded. If you come across any errors or discrepancies, please make a note of them and send them to our publishing office. We are constantly updating our manuscripts, eliminating errors, and improving quality.

Please contact us at the address above.

About the Cookbook Delights Series

The *Cookbook Delights Series* includes many different topics and themes. If you have a passion for food and wish to know more information about different foods, then this series of cookbooks will be beneficial to you. Each book features a different type of food, such as avocados, strawberries, huckleberries, salmon, vegetarian, lentils, almonds, cherries, coconuts, lemons, and many, many more.

The *Cookbook Delights Series* not only includes cookbooks about individual foods but also includes several holiday-themed cookbooks. Whatever your favorite holiday may be, chances are we have a cookbook with recipes designed with that holiday in mind. Some examples include *Halloween Delights, Thanksgiving Delights, Christmas Delights, Valentine Delights, Mother's Day Delights, St. Patrick's Day Delights,* and *Easter Delights.*

Each cookbook is designed for easy use and is organized into alphabetical sections. Over 250 recipes are included along with other interesting facts, folklore, and history of the featured food or theme. Each book comes with a beautiful full-color cover, ordering information, and a list of other upcoming books in the series.

Note cards, bookmarks, and a daily journal have been printed and are available to go along with each cookbook. You may view the entire line of cookbooks, journals, cards, posters, puzzles, and bookmarks by visiting our website at www.christmasdelights.net, or you can email us with your questions and your comments to: sales@whisperingpinepress.com.

Please ask your local bookstore to carry these sets of books.

To order, please contact:

Whispering Pine Press International, Inc.
c/o Christmas Delights Cookbook
P.O. Box 214, Spokane Valley, WA 99037-0214
Phone: (509) 928-8700 | Fax: (509) 922-9949
Email: sales@whisperingpinepress.com
Publisher Websites: www.WhisperingPinePress.com
www.WhisperingPinePressBookstore.com
Blog: www.WhisperingPinePressBlog.com
SAN 253-200X

We Invite You to Join the
Whispering Pine Press International, Inc.,
Book Club

Whispering Pine Press International, Inc.
c/o Christmas Delights Cookbook
P.O. Box 214, Spokane Valley, WA 99037-0214
Phone: (509) 928-8700 | Fax: (509) 922-9949
Email: sales@whisperingpinepress.com
Publisher Websites: www.WhisperingPinePress.com
www.WhisperingPinePressBookstore.com
Blog: www.WhisperingPinePressBlog.com

Buy 11 books and get the next one free, based on the average price of the first eleven purchased.

How the club works:

Simply use the order form below and order books from our catalog. You can buy just one at a time or all eleven at once. After the first eleven books are purchased, the next one is free. Please add shipping and handling as listed on this form. There are no purchase requirements at any time during your membership. Free book credit is based on the average price of the first eleven books purchased.

Join today. Pick your books and mail in the form today.

Yes. I want to join the Whispering Pine Press International, Inc., Book Club. Enroll me and send the books indicated below.

Title   Price

1. _____
2. _____
3. _____
4. _____
5. _____
6. _____
7. _____
8. _____
9. _____
10. _____
11. _____

Free Book Title: _____

Free Book Price: _____ Avg. Price: _____ Total Price: _____

Credit for the free book is based on the average price of the first 11 books purchased.

(Circle one) Check | Visa | MasterCard | Discover | American Express

Credit Card #: _____ Expiration Date: _____

Name: _____

Address: _____

City: _____ State: _____ Country: _____

Zip/Postal: _____ Phone: (_____) _____

Email: _____

Signature _____

318

Whispering Pine Press International, Inc. Fundraising Opportunities

Fundraising cookbooks are proven moneymakers and great keepsake providers for your group. Whispering Pine Press International, Inc., offers a very special personalized cookbook fundraising program that encourages success to organizations all across the USA.

Our prices are competitive and fair. Currently, we offer a special of 100 books with many free features and excellent customer service. Any purchase you make is guaranteed first-rate.

Flexibility is not a problem. If you have special needs, we guarantee our cooperation in meeting each of them. Our goal is to create a cookbook that goes beyond your expectations. We have the confidence and a record that promises continual success.

Another great fundraising program is the *Cookbook Delights Series* Program. With cookbook orders of 50 copies or more, your organization receives a huge discount, making for a prompt and lucrative solution.

We also specialize in assisting group fundraising – Christian, community, nonprofit, and academic among them. If you are struggling for a new idea, something that will enhance your success and broaden your appeal, Whispering Pine Press International, Inc., can help.

For more information, write, phone, or fax to:

Whispering Pine Press International, Inc.
P.O. Box 214
Spokane Valley, WA 99037-0214
Phone: (509) 928-8700 | Fax: (509) 922-9949
Email: sales@whisperingpinepress.com
Publisher Websites: www.WhisperingPinePress.com
www.WhisperingPinePressBookstore.com
Blog: www.WhisperingPinePressBlog.com
Book Website: www.ChristmasDelights.net
SAN 253-200X

Personalized and/or Translated Order Form for Any Book by Whispering Pine Press International, Inc.

Dear Readers:

If you or your organization wishes to have this book or any other of our books personalized, we will gladly accommodate your needs. For instance, if you would like to change the names of the characters in a book to the names of the children in your family or Sunday school class, we would be happy to work with you on such a project. We can add more information of your choosing and customize this book especially for your family, group, or organization.

We are also offering an option of translating your book into another language. Please fill out the form below telling us exactly how you would like us to personalize your book.

Please send your request to:

Whispering Pine Press International, Inc.
c/o Christmas Delights Cookbook
P.O. Box 214, Spokane Valley, WA 99037-0214
Phone: (509) 928-8700 | Fax: (509) 922-9949
Email: sales@whisperingpinepress.com
Publisher Websites: www.WhisperingPinePress.com
www.WhisperingPinePressBookstore.com
Blog: www.WhisperingPinePressBlog.com

Person/Organization placing request: _____

_____ Date: _____

Phone: (____) _____ Fax: (____)_____

Address: _____

City: _____ State: _____ Zip: _____

Language of the book: _____

Please explain your request in detail: _____

_____

_____

_____

_____

Christmas Delights Cookbook

A Collection of Christmas Recipes

How to Order

Get your additional copies of this book by returning an order form
and your check, money order, or credit card information to:

Whispering Pine Press International, Inc.
c/o Christmas Delights Cookbook
P.O. Box 214, Spokane Valley, WA 99037-0214
Phone: (509) 928-8700 | Fax: (509) 922-9949
Email: sales@whisperingpinepress.com
Publisher Websites: www.WhisperingPinePress.com
www.WhisperingPinePressBookstore.com
Blog: www.WhisperingPinePressBlog.com

Customer Name: _____

Address: _____

City, St., Zip: _____

Phone/Fax: _____

Email: _____

- -

Please send me _____ copies of _____

_____ at $_____

per copy and $4.95 for shipping and handling per book, plus

$2.95 each for additional books. Enclosed is my check, money

order, or charge my account for $_____.

☐ Check   ☐ Money Order   ☐ Credit Card

(*Circle One*) MasterCard | Discover | Visa | American Express
☐☐☐☐   ☐☐☐☐   ☐☐☐☐   ☐☐☐☐

Expiration Date: _____

_____
Signature

_____
Print Name

Print Name

321

Whispering Pine Press International, Inc.
Your Northwest Book Publishing Company
P.O. Box 214
Spokane Valley, WA 99037-0214 USA
Phone: (509) 928-8700 | Fax: (509) 922-9949
Email: sales@whisperingpinepress.com
Publisher Websites: www.WhisperingPinePress.com
www.WhisperingPinePressBookstore.com

Shop Online:
www.whisperingpinepressbookstore.com
Fax orders to: (509)922-9949

Gift-wrapping, Autographing, and Inscription
We are proud to offer personal autographing by the author. For a limited time this service is absolutely free!
Gift-wrapping is also available for $4.95 per item.

1. Sold To
Name: _____
Street/Route: _____
_____
City: _____
State: _____ Zip: _____
Country: _____
Gift message: _____
_____
Email address: _____
Daytime Phone: (_ _ _) _ _ _-_ _ _ _
　*Necessary for verifying orders
　Home Phone: (_ _ _) _ _ _-_ _ _ _
　Fax: (_ _ _) _ _ _-_ _ _ _

2. Ship To
☐ Is this a new or corrected address?
☐ Alternative Shipping Address
☐ Mailing Address

Name: _____
Address: _____
_____
City: _____
State: _____ Zip: _____
Country: _____
Email address: _____

3. Items Ordered

ISBN # /Item #	Size	Color	Qty.	Title or Description	Price	Total

4. Method Of Payment

☐ Visa ☐ MasterCard ☐ Discover ☐ American Express
☐ Check/Money Order　Please make it payable to Whispering Pine Press
International, Inc. (No Cash or COD's)

Expiration Date

Account Number _____ / _____
Month　Year

☐☐☐☐ ☐☐☐☐ ☐☐☐☐ ☐☐☐☐

Signature_____
　　　　　Cardholder's signature
Printed Name_____
　　　　　Please print name of cardholder
Address of Cardholder_____
_____

5. Shipping & Handling

Continental US
US Postal Ground: For books please add $4.95 for the first book and $2.95 each for additional books. All non-book items, add 15% of the Subtotal. Please allow 1-4 weeks for delivery.
US Postal Air: Please add $15.00 shipping and handling. Please allow 1-3 days for delivery.

Alaska, Hawaii, and the US Territories
By Ship: Please add 10% shipping and handling (minimum charge $15.00). Please allow 6-12 weeks for delivery.
By Air: Please add 12% shipping and handling (minimum charge $15.00). Please allow 2-6 weeks for delivery.

International
By Ship: Please add 10% shipping and handling (minimum charge $15.00). Please allow 6-12 weeks for delivery.
By Air: Please add 12% shipping and handling (minimum charge $15.00). Please allow 2-6 weeks for delivery.
FedEx Shipments: Add $5.00 to the above airmail charges for overnight delivery.

Subtotal	
Gift wrap $4.95 Each	
For delivery in WA add 8.7% sales tax.	
Shipping See chart at left	
6. Total	

322

About the Author and Cook

Karen Jean Matsko Hood has always enjoyed cooking, baking, and experimenting with recipes. At this time Hood is working to complete a series of cookbooks that blends her skills and experience in cooking and entertaining. Hood entertains large groups of people and especially enjoys designing creative menus with holiday, international, ethnic, and regional themes.

Hood is publishing a cookbook series entitled the Cookbook Delights Series, in which each cookbook emphasizes a different food ingredient or theme. The first cookbook in the series is Apple Delights Cookbook. Hood is working to complete another series of cookbooks titled Hood and Matsko Family Cookbooks, which includes many recipes handed down from her family heritage and others that have emerged from more current family traditions. She has been invited to speak on talk radio shows on various topics, and favorite recipes from her cookbooks have been prepared on local television programs.

Hood was born and raised in Great Falls, Montana. As an undergraduate, she attended the College of St. Benedict in St. Joseph, Minnesota, and St. John's University in Collegeville, Minnesota. She attended the University of Great Falls in Great Falls, Montana. Hood received a B.S. Degree in Natural Science from the College of St. Benedict and minored in both Psychology and Secondary Education. Upon her graduation, Hood and her husband taught science and math on the island of St. Croix in the U.S. Virgin Islands. Hood has completed postgraduate classes at the University of Iowa in Iowa City, Iowa. In May 2001, she completed her Master's Degree in Pastoral Ministry at Gonzaga University in Spokane, Washington. She has taken postgraduate classes at Lewis and Clark College on the North Idaho college campus in Coeur d'Alene, Idaho, Taylor University in Fort Wayne, Indiana, Spokane Falls Community College, Spokane Community College, Washington State University, University of Washington, and Eastern Washington University. Hood is working on research projects to complete her Ph.D. in Leadership Studies at Gonzaga University in Spokane, Washington.

Hood resides in Greenacres, Washington, along with her husband, many of her seventeen children, and foster children. Her interests include writing, research, and teaching. She previously has volunteered as a court advocate in the Spokane juvenile court system for abused and neglected children. Hood is a literary advocate for youth and adults. Her hobbies include cooking, baking, collecting, photography, indoor and outdoor gardening, farming, and the cultivation of unusual flowering plants and orchids. She enjoys raising several specialty breeds of animals including Babydoll Southdown, Friesen, and Icelandic sheep, Icelandic horses, bichons frisés, cockapoos, Icelandic sheepdogs, a Newfoundland, a Rottweiler, a variety of Nubian and fainting goats, and a few rescue cats. Hood also enjoys bird-watching and finds all aspects of nature precious.

She demonstrates a passionate appreciation of the environment and a respect for all life. She also invites you to visit her websites:

www.KarenJeanMatskoHood.com
www.KarenJeanMatskoHoodBookstore.com
www.KarenJeanMatskoHoodBlog.com
www.KarensKidsBooks.com
www.KarensTeenBooks.com

www.HoodFamilyBlog.com
www.HoodFamily.com

Author's Social Media
Like or Friend the Author on Facebook:
https://www.facebook.com/KarenJeanMatskoHoodAuthorFanPage
Follow the Author on Twitter: https://twitter.com/KarenJeanHood
Google Plus Profile: http://google.com/+KarenJeanMatskoHood
Pinterest: https://www.pinterest.com/KarenJMHood/
LinkedIn: http://www.linkedin.com/in/KarenJeanMatskoHood
YouTube: http://www.youtube.com/KarenJeanMatskoHood
Instagram: http://instagram.com/KarenJeanMatskoHood
MySpace: https://myspace.com/KarenJeanMatskoHood

www.ingramcontent.com/pod-product-compliance
Lightning Source LLC
Chambersburg PA
CBHW031235090426

42742CB00007B/207